Isaac Walker

Dress

As it has Been, is and Will Be

Isaac Walker

Dress
As it has Been, is and Will Be

ISBN/EAN: 9783337139827

Printed in Europe, USA, Canada, Australia, Japan

Cover: Foto ©Andreas Hilbeck / pixelio.de

More available books at **www.hansebooks.com**

So sweet a kiss the golden sun gives not
To those fresh morning drops upon the rose,
As thy eye-beams —*Love's Labour Lost.*

THE Master said: "Where the solid qualities are in excess of accomplishments, we have rusticity. Where the accomplishments are in excess of the solid qualities, we have the manners of a clerk. Where the accomplishments and solid qualities are equally blended, we then have the man of complete virtue."

CONFUCIUS. (*Chinese Classics.*)

"To dwell in the wide house of the world, to stand in the correct seat of the world, and to walk in the great path of the world .. to be above the power of riches and honors, of poverty and mean condition, and of power and force .... these characteristics constitute the great man."

MENCIUS. (*Chinese Classics.*)

"They who are first informed should instruct those who are later in being informed, and they who first apprehend principles should instruct those who are slower in doing so."

MENCIUS. (*Chinese Classics.*)

DRESS:

As It Has Been,
Is,
And Will Be.

DESCRIBING WITH PARTICULARITY RECENT INNOVA-
TIONS, AND FORECASTING THE TENDENCY OF
MALE DRAPERY FROM WHAT WE KNOW,

.

TOGETHER WITH ALL THAT IS PRACTICAL TO-DAY.

By *ISAAC WALKER.*

NEW YORK:
ISAAC WALKER, 275 FIFTH AVENUE.
1885.

INTRODUCTORY.

In preparing this volume for publication, the author has sought to present in serious language the aspect of the varying costumes of mankind throughout history, until the present day, from a purely artistic standpoint. The time, he believes, is ripe for such a treatise, written, as this one has been, in a conscientious vein, and embodying the experience of a life-time in the designing and making of men's outer-wear, both in England and the United States. And the author has been the more prompted to undertake this semi-professional task because he has noted the rapid changes in taste, both as to fabrics and ideals of style which are to be seen throughout the Union. The great houses that used to flourish on the trade of the *élite* are swiftly passing away, and giving place to those proficient in the highest forms

of art; while immense manufacturing establishments turn out cheap material and ill-
fitting garments for the multitude.

In the advanced line of merchant tailoring
are now found elegantly appointed shops,
filled with imported goods of only the first
qualities. In these establishments a man is
not dressed in a minute, but his peculiarities
of frame are made the subject of careful
study, and his adaptability to special styles
and colors is seen in the light of experience
and cultivated judgment.

However these pages may impress the
reader, it cannot be controverted that in
general and detail, *truth*, and a sincere wish
to elevate the art of becoming attire, have
been the only aims of the author.

Isaac Walker,

No. 275 Fifth avenue.

N. Y., Oct. 1, 1885.

CHAPTER I.

In the mind of the future historian a new movement in the social life of America will always date from the close of the civil war. That bloody conflict roused the continent from an era of supine and peaceful life, from a period of hum-drum and homely lethargy into an eager ambition to start on a fresh march toward a higher civilization implying loftier standards of literature and art—in fine, more imposing architecture, better schools of painting and sculpture, a finer taste in male and female costume, and an indulgence in those refined luxuries which always follow on the elevation of the national manhood, and the sudden growth of large fortunes. This is not true of the United States alone, but will be found in the mutations of European States as well, and is perhaps nowhere better exemplified than in the triumph of the German arms in 1870–71; the founding of an empire the greatest since the Cæsars ruled in

Rome, and the consequent stamp of a prouder
and more independent individuality on the
Teutonic mind. And with this assertion of
indomitable self in the nationalities wherever found, comes the determination to exhibit its sign-manual in an outward form, and,
primarily, that is, in dress. Who will say that
the American gentleman of the period since
1865, is not one of much more culture in
matters of art than he of the ante-bellum
days? Who will say that the American of
1885, of whatever social grade, is not a much
better dressed man than corresponding generations before the war? And the traveler
in Germany will find, too, that in the fifteen
years that have elapsed since the sanguinary
struggle with France, Teutonic attire has improved in style and fabric to an astonishing
degree. This all comes from the sudden rise
in the national tone, the same transition, for
example, that is apparent in the conditions of
a man poor at the one extreme and rich at the
other. But in no country of the world, of
this or any other time, has the advance from
a slovenly habit of dress to one of elegance
and good taste been as swift to the ulti-

matum as in the United States. This progress we see, too, not only on the Atlantic
sea-board, but, traveling westward by easy
stations, we behold a total change for the
better in the last twenty years, showing that
the art of dressing well has kept pace with
those hand-maids of art, music and the drama,
in the leading cities and towns of the interior.
Is there any other proof necessary to demon-
strate that costuming the man in the prevailing garb of the day demands as fine a conception and application of the rules of high
art as this very circumstance of the invasion
of the interior cities of America by a superior
kind of culture? Before the war it was rare
to find a place of 20,000 inhabitants with a
theatre or opera-house, but now there is
scarcely a place numbering half this population which has not its finely appointed house
for lyric and dramatic display, whereas formerly the old-fashioned hall, with wooden
benches, perched on the top of the town's
loftiest warehouse, was the place of amuse-
ment whither the goodly folk repaired for intellectual recreation.

The almost universal use of the piano, the

vast volume of inter-State tiavel, the annual pilgrimages to metropolitan centres, and last, but not least, the yearly visits of hundreds of thousands of Americans to Europe, have leavened the masses and cosmopolized this people until it may be said that, taken as a whole, Americans are the best clad people in the world. It is a curious study, too, to note the movement by which this has been accomplished, if we leave for a moment out of consideration the great cities. Take our city of twenty thousand inhabitants, as before. A score of years ago fine dress suits could hardly be found among the whole population. That was when it was not churchmanlike to go to the play, or in pursuit of pleasure to travel beyond the Calvinistic notion of enjoyment. Opera *bouffe* had no countenance in those days. *Patience, Pinafore,* and *The Mikado* would have been driven penniless from the town by the potent breath of the pulpit; whereas now the strains of the latest lyric compositions sung on the local boards are heard issuing from many households of the town. And not only this, but the youth of both sexes delight in talking art and prac-

ticing it also to a limited extent; private
theatricals reign in the local assemblies, and

·*1861.*·   ·*1885*·

costuming in character is cultivated by the
young of both sexes. Is there any one so

blind as not to see that this typical town of
America is a highly interesting social micro-
cosm in itself, presenting an abundant field
for philosophical study, as showing healthy
advances in culture at last culminating in
that art which seems the last to command respect, but when once mastered is the last to
be lost—*dress?*   And let us note, too, that a
man who has once known, and has been thoroughly in sympathy with, *good* suitable attire,
will never abandon it, save commanded by a
resistless fate.   Fine eating, good wine, cards,
horses, athletic sports, and boon companions
will all go before the surrender of the garments which have made him a central figure
of his circle.   And thus it has come about
that in our typical inland city, where formerly the gentry would appear in their old-
fashioned " broad-cloths," with street boots
and colored ties, we now see at an evening
party seven-eighths of the males attired in
dress suits and the conventional wear on the
feet and about the neck.   This transformation has arisen from the causes named, and
has emancipated the communities from in-
sular narrowness, and given the local life a

metropolitan flavor. We might here well pause to inquire what moral effect has this radical change within a generation wrought on the youth of the community in our mind's eye? It must be patent to all. With the majority of the young men there the dress suit is the most priceless possession, for instead of being compelled to spend his evenings in beer halls or billiard saloons, or in evil associations, he feels that he can seek refuge in ladies' society, and be on a par with the wealthier and more aristocratic of the town. He feels that, so costumed, he is a gentleman who must doff the manners of the shop and the street for those of refinement and the drawing-room. Nor is there any considerable disproportion between this progress in the one particular mentioned and the elevation of the standard of general dress in such communities. When sufficiently cultivated, the young man feels that his wear must be custom made, instead of a hap-hazard selection from those great stocks of alleged clothing which flood the country from establishments patterned, as it were, on the manufactories of Birmingham and Manchester, making goods for the colonies with every implication that the inhabitants were savages. One of these suits of clothing suggests that a bale of sham wool has been thrown into a hopper and that thirty seconds thereafter trousers, coat, and waistcoat pop forth from the delivery all neatly pressed and folded, and quite ready to adorn the rural frame.

This barbarous prevalence of ready-made clothing will, however, pass away as years go on, as shams and shoddies disappear from our social life, and when that universal nuisance in art, the " patentee," is an obsolete factor. This tendency is already marked, for who now is seen wearing a paper collar— once the pride of the multitudinous clerk— the wood-pulp shirt-front, or the cork hat? Of course, we are speaking of the hamlet, the village, and the town, for these inventions never invaded the better circles of men of the Atlantic sea-board. The spread of such an invention in the inland territory can be accounted for on several grounds. First: All of those false proverbs and unfortunate sayings, which come from the average self-made man; and by this we do not wish to be understood as speaking lightly of those who have hewn out, with their unaided hands and brains, their fortunes and their fame, for they are the true aristocrats of mankind. But there is an idea in the mind of the hardy toiler who has risen to wealth and influence, that to be well and artistically attired is to be foppish, shallow, and effeminate. Severity in style, ill fit, coarse cloth, and well-worn raiment, among these men, usually deform a majestic carriage and a strong and intellectual countenance. We consider this to be the result either of neglect or affectation. Should it follow that because the empty-pated idler who strolls our streets, on little better than mechanic's wages, concentrates all of his thought on his outward garb, that the external appearance of a commanding figure is not worthy of a passing thought by its possessor? It doubtless made Horace Greeley notorious as he wished to carefully adjust his well-worn stock under his left ear, and distribute a shabby pantaloon in a cow-hide boot. But how much better would he have appeared to the eye and to posterity, if he had dressed in the clothes of a gentleman, and appeared among his followers with these baneful pretenses left out! Men like Horace Greeley, exercising as they have, and do, a vast influence on their followers, have contributed much to retard healthful and artistic dressing in America. Ignorantly laboring against the truism of Pope, that

" **Dress makes the man ; the want of it the fellow,**"

they instilled a retrograde movement as to attire in the rural mind, now happily passing away. It would seem, too, that the American intellect, generally keen, active, and alert, in its average development, would have learned at least the commercial importance of perfection in the style of dress of this commercial age. But it has not, notwithstanding the very obvious fact that a shabbily dressed man has all the odds against him in the race in life. Given two men, the one slow of thought, destitute of personal magnetism, devoid of culture, yet a tastefully dressed manikin, and the other quick to perceive, with strong powers of brain, and attractive physical gifts, but with ill-suited and

noticeably bad apparel, and in the business
centres of finance or the Exchange, or the
busy marts of commerce, and the former has
every advantage, reaping harvest after harvest, to the dismay of the man of manlier
purpose and vigor and superior mental development. Strange it is, that this palpable
truth is ignored so widely in a country whose
corner-stone is the almighty dollar. Leaving
entirely out of sight the many social and
amatory advantages which correct dressing
gives to the man, with all of the keen delight of associations at the club and by the
fireside, it is often incomprehensible that
clear-headed men will go on, year after year,
in apparent ignorance that there is such a
person as a tailor in all the land. And yet
we find it in those very walks of life where
it least ought to be—among professional men,
whose culture and good taste most assuredly
ought to be beyond question.

CHAPTER II.

PHILOSOPHERS have not yet been able to agree upon a proper definition of the word *man*, all the forms so far proposed being ob- noxious to the reproach of omitting quite as much that is characteristic as they convey. From Plato's two-legged animal without feathers down to the Wall-street definition of man as a being that sells short, there is no entirely satisfactory rendering of the name. This being admitted, it is not, perhaps, too much to say that when we define man as a creature able to wear and to comprehend the significance of dress, we have come near to a correct appreciation of his relative import- ance in the universe.

When we observe the lower animals, we find that, as they approach the higher type, they are seen to take pleasure in personal ap- parel. The wild horse of the plains of South America, or the steppes of Tartary, has a free and noble bearing; but how much more eloquent of developed intelligence and conscious personal worth is the spirited motion of the war-horse, treading proudly to the martial music and the sound of his warlike trappings, and playing with the ringing chains of his bit ! The distance between the two is as great and as clearly defined as that between an Indian brave and the Prime Minister of a great empire. Carlyle has done well to insist on the immense importance of clothes as an expression of the over soul in man ; and it is to be hoped that the hints he has thrown out for a philosophy of this great subject may one day be expanded by some competent thinker, and wrought into a harmonious and synthetic whole.

All the early records of mankind agree as to the probable origin of clothes. The primitive man is always seen to be content with the fell furnished him by nature, even after he has learned to fabricate weapons more or less rude. Not till he feels the first dim movements of taste awakened within him by the contemplation of the colors in the skins of his four-footed fellows does he begin to think of adorning his person, and strutting, like the jay in the fable, in borrowed plumes. It may be regarded as a settled point, that the first use of clothes was not for warmth or protection, but wholly for ornamentation, or, in a word, for dress, properly so called in contradistinction to the secondary and derivative purpose of clothing as a covering against weather. A careful study of the myths and legends of the race leaves no doubt on this point. With the skin the savage naturally took to himself the name of the animal he had stripped; and here we come upon the germ of a true hierarchy of costume, the rude beginning, indeed, of the gorgeous and complex court splendors of Egypt and Assyria, of Rome and of Byzantium.

The earliest monuments of Egypt show us the first steps toward a systematic attire. The garment is but a linen cloth around the loins, with the skin of a leopard worn on the shoulders. This was in 1600 B. C. Gradually the dress becomes fuller and more elaborate; and the distinctions of social position, marked in the earlier times by so simple a device as the doubling of the linen folds about the middle, are shown by richer stuffs,

by various colors, by added skirts and collars.
The king was recognized by his crown,

called the *pshent*, often nearly resembling a
mitre, and by a triangular projecting skirt of

leather, ornamented with gold. The dress of the lower classes was chiefly of wool, a material little used by the higher orders, except as an outer covering, their robes being mostly of *byblus*, a mixture of linen and cotton, or of linen, which the kings chose exclusively. The finest sort was known as royal linen, and was very high-priced. In the story of Satni-Khâmoïs, the couches and beds of Thouboui's palace are spread with royal linen.*

The Assyrian ordinary dress was a robe with a long skirt and short sleeves. There seems to have been no essential difference in the form of the women's dress. Upper garments were not allowed to any below the priestly rank. The king wore a long robe or skirt, and over this a mantle with heavy fringes. The monuments show that the Assyrians possessed remarkable skill in weaving and embroidering all manner of stuffs; and the Bible is full of allusions to the rich colors and tracery of their garments, "exceeding in dyed attire, all of them princes to look to."

The Phœnicians undoubtedly learned from

---

* Maspéro. Contes Egyptiens.

the Assyrians and Babylonians the arts of dyeing and embroidery, which they carried to such great perfection, both in their cities on the Syrian coast and in Carthage, their greatest colony, and their costume, so far as we are enabled to judge by the fragmentary remains of their civilization, seems to have resembled the Assyrian rather than the Egyptian in its general features. The Etruscans, whose origin is still a matter of uncertainty, have so many points of resemblance with the Eastern nations of antiquity, that, while we cannot exactly describe their costume, we can see that it was in some respects like that of the Egyptians, though it is known that some features of the Roman dress, such as the *toga picta*, the *tunica palmata*, the *prætexta*, and the rich sandals, were of Etruscan origin. The luxury of this people was very famous in antiquity, and they were especially given to indulgences of the table, with every accompaniment of costly perfumes, crowns, embroidered couches, and rich robes. The *obesi Etrusci* are frequently met with in the Roman poets.

The dress of the ancient Jews always

showed the influence of one or the other of
the great empires to which, in turn, the
chosen people became subject; and even in
the brief intervals during which the nation
was politically independent, there was no
revolt from the dominant taste in dress.
There were close under-garments, with an
over-tunic, worn by both sexes, the tunic being much the same as the modern *Kaftan*
of the East, with a large outer mantle, like
a cloak, gathered in at the waist by a girdle,
as needed; and these outer robes were often
ornamented very richly. The attire of the
priesthood, and especially that of the high
priest, was costly and magnificent. The monuments of Egypt and Assyria, from which
we might have expected illustrations of the
Jewish national costume, leave us very much
in the dark, the Hebrews figuring in these
records as captives, stripped of their outer
clothing and their ornaments; and our real
sources of information on this interesting subject are the writings of Isaiah and Ezekiel.

One general characteristic marks all the
Oriental costumes, both of antiquity and
of modern times—the flowing outer robes,

which lend so much dignity to the stature and the bearing of even the meanest man. A garment so inconsistent with haste and active physical exertion could only be found in countries and among social organizations too settled in manners and habits to accept the idea of business as the chief end of life. To the Oriental of three thousand years ago, as to the Turk or the Persian of to-day, the day is evidently sufficient unto itself, and the morrow will be like to-day. His *kismet*, or destiny, is written on his forehead, no less for this fleeting earthly existence than for the future immortality, and he goes calmly about his affairs with none of the European impatience; for he well knows that, if not this hour, then the next will bring him to his journey's end, or to the attainment of his object, if it is to be attained; and, if it is not, that must be as God pleases.

The profound religious sense of the Eastern races, and the dignity and power of their priesthood, have combined to give a family likeness and an unchanging form to their national costumes. Two Eastern races contradict this general law—the Japanese and

the Chinese. The Japanese are now undergoing a rapid process of transformation in
habits of thought and in manners, from the
contact, too suddenly and violently brought
about, with European ideas and modes of
life. What they were in the past, the Chinese—their teachers and exemplars—still are,
and are likely long to be; and, strangely
enough, we find in this extraordinary people
a prevailing style of costume older, indeed,
in its origin than the civilization of Greece
and Rome, and yet wholly in sympathy with
the business ideas and habits that have so
greatly simplified the dress of modern Europe. A peaceful, active, ingenious, and in-
dustrious people, the Chinese have found it
necessary to move freely about their commercial and agricultural affairs, to be ready
always to thread their way from one end of
their vast cities to the other through narrow
streets and jostling multitudes; and their in-
clination to trade and the affairs of life, a
natural outcome of their practical genius, has
been sharpened and stimulated by the competition forced upon every individual in the
struggle for a livelihood in the midst of a

population so vast. To be unincumbered in his movements was, therefore, the first necessity for the Chinese, and no costume known among men so entirely leaves the wearer free in all his motions as the easy, firmly-fastened shoes, the loose yet close trousers, and the short outer shirt, with open neck, almost universal among the people of China. Yet the Chinese are well aware of the advantage to be derived from a rich and stately official costume; and their great dignitaries and wealthy men could hold their own for splendid and appropriate dress in any Court of Europe or the East.

The classical costume of Greece and Rome is familiar to every one, in the reproductions of the statues and works of art that have come down to us, and in the numberless paintings, the works of great artists, like Gérôme and Alma Tadema, that have brought before us the scenes of Roman and Greek daily life. One feature is common to the classical costume and the Oriental—the general, flowing outline, which shows that the wearer is master of his own time, and impelled by no stern necessities to personal activity. For the Greek and the Roman the business of life was to meet in the public places, to discuss the political and military events of the day, to hear Pericles or Cicero explaining or attacking a line of policy, or pleading his own cause, to be borne in his litter or his chariot to a great feast, or to order the purchase of a villa or a family of slaves. The work of the classical world was done by the slaves; and the citizens were, practically, nobles, administering, through agents, estates more or less important. To such men personal ease was inseparable from the idea of freedom, as opposed to the condition of those on whom lay the burden of daily toil; and the flowing costume was, therefore. the privilege and the badge of nobility. The indignation and disgust of Augustus Cæsar when, seeing the Forum crowded with workingmen and slaves in their short garments, to the exclusion of the typical Roman toga, he broke out with the line from Virgil,

En—
Romanos rerum dominos, gentem que togatam ?
" Are these your Romans, lords of the world and the men
    of the toga ?"

show, as in a photograph, the gulf between the Roman citizens, whose care was empire, and the toiling multitude below them.

The toga was to hold its place for a good while after this; but the distinctive garment of the Europeans of to-day, the trousers, had already come into view as a part of respect-able attire in the third century. This part of the costume was familiar to the Romans as peculiar to the Gauls and Germans; but its adoption by the conquering race dates from the wars with the Persians, to whom also this form of dress was national.

After the fall of the Empire, it is not easy to trace the general styles of costume in Western Europe. The Eastern Empire main-tained and developed almost a new system of civil costume, by adopting ideas from the Oriental world, and combining the Persian costume with the Roman; but in the West, after the temporary revival under Charle-magne, the distinctive Roman costume dis-appeared from the general view, remaining local in some parts of Italy.

CHAPTER III.

THE rise of feudalism brought in entirely new ideas on costume in civil life. In the Church, however, the traditions of antiquity survived and underwent comparatively slight changes under the influence of the new social organization.

The monastic orders used much the same form of dress, with sufficient differences of color and head-dress to make the order of the wearer recognizable. The Universities had also their special costumes, generally long, flowing gowns, with capes and hoods, the same, at first, for the doctors and the bachelors, though later on a distinction was established between the dresses of the two.

Under the feudal system, the dependence of the vassals was marked by the form of dress, or by some badge worn either em-broidered or painted on the stuff of the outer dress, or in the shape of a collar. Further devices came in with the growth of industries, and the rise of the great trading towns. The guilds of merchants and manufacturers took as much delight in the science of heraldry as the feudal lords, and with the sense of their power and importance, as they increased in wealth, asserted their dignity by the wearing of appropriate devices and emblems. The variety in style and design of dress was a characteristic of the communities in which feudalism had most firmly taken root. Thus, the cities of Northern and Central Italy, where feudalism had almost no representation in the presence of the municipal traditions of antiquity, never at any time really extinct, made a less splendid display, in this respect, than the cities of Germany, Flanders and France; and it is in the monuments of these countries that what is properly called mediæval costume is to be studied. In England there are interesting memorials of dress from the Anglo Saxon period down to the present time. The dress of the Anglo-Saxons was composed of a tunic, generally short, partly open at the sides, and confined about the waist by a girdle. Over this was worn a mantle or cloak. The legs were covered with drawers fitting close to the lower leg, like hose, which were ornamented by bands crossed like those of Malvolio in the play. Extra mantles were added against the severity of the weather, and a hood covered the head

The Normans introduced a richer style of costume, but they adopted also the tunic and amplified it. They extended also the use of rich and costly furs on their outer garments.

A type of the richest form of the modified Norman dress is seen in the monument of King John, in Worcester Cathedral. He is represented here as clad in a loose tunic, reaching to his ankles. The sleeves are tight on the arms. Over this tunic is a full-sleeved crimson dalmatic, richly embroidered with gold, and held about the waist by a girdle, with a long pendant end. The mantle worn over these hangs down the back, and is gathered about the right arm. The hose are red, and the boots black, with knightly spurs of gold. This costume was essentially the one worn by the knights and nobles of the period. It is to be remembered that the military spirit which made war the only fitting em-

ployment of a well-born man, showed itself
as much in the wearing of armor, even in
time of peace, as in the love of heraldic devices
and badges for the retainers of the baron,
and most of the effigies on the tombs of the
Middle Ages are represented dressed as if for
war. The growth of luxury, and the taste for
refinements in life, which came in with the
later Crusades, after the Western warriors had
become acquainted with the higher Saracen
civilization, display their influence as markedly
in the comparative disuse of the warlike costume as in the introduction of more costly
stuffs and forms of attire directly traceable
to Eastern ideas. These changes lead the inquirer out of the Middle Age, into the most
picturesque period of European costume, the
Sixteenth Century.

CHAPTER IV.

At the opening of the sixteenth century there is apparent in Europe a movement of change in the variety and in the character of the costumes. In great part this is due to the changed conditions of warfare consequent on the invention of gunpowder, and its application to fire-arms. The shields and coats of plate and of mail were more and more seen to be an incumbrance and an additional danger to the wearer, and, though they were still worn at times by individuals, and even by bodies of troops, there was a growing belief in their uselessness, and a conviction that their day was over. With the defensive armor went the modifications of costume that had grown out of its use as the recognized mark of knighthood and gentle birth, and there was a tendency toward the assimilation of the civil and the military dress, in their main features. With the defensive armor there went also the comparative im-

portance of the knights in battle. The Swiss
and the Spanish infantry became the main
strength of the army, and the last apparent
reason for the maintenance of the feudal
organization of society was called finally in
question. Many of the infinite subdivisions
of caste in civil life, each one marked by its
peculiar and invariable style of dress, disappeared, one after another, as the burghers became more important and gathered into their
body men who sought the security of the
towns and the protection of the growing
guilds. The handicrafts tended to coalesce
as they were more or less intimately connected, and the members of a guild, pursuing
related industries, became known by a similar
style of costume. The increase of wealth, and
its wide diffusion, had even a more important
influence upon dress, for nothing is more
democratic or leveling than wealth. What
the upper classes wear, the men of an inferior
class will aim at wearing, as they obtain command of means. The only serious obstacle
in the way of a more rapid unification of the
social elements at the beginning of the
sixteenth century was the still defiant atti-

tude of feudalism, which made every effort to maintain the existing institutions; but the active forces, the spirit of adventure, the thirst for discovery, the restless commercial enterprise, were all against it. The tendency was toward the breaking up of the arbitrary divisions in society, and, consequently, against the divergences in costume which made of each class a kind of community by itself. The dress of modern times, the dress which to-day marks the civilized man in every quarter of the globe, may be said to have come in with the sixteenth century. M. Paul Lacroix (le bibliophile Jacob) in his valuable history of this period, writes as follows: " We find that a distinct separation between ancient and modern dress took place as early as the sixteenth century. In fact, our present fashions may be said to have taken their origin from about that time. It was during this century that men adopted clothes closely fitting to the body—overcoats with tight sleeves, felt hats with more or less wide brims, and close boots and shoes. The women also wore their dresses closely fitting to the figure, with tight sleeves, low-crowned hats, and richly trimmed petticoats. These garments, which differ altogether from those of antiquity, constitute, as it were, the common type from which have arisen the endless varieties of modern male and female dress; and there is no doubt then that fashion will be continually moving backward and forward from period to period, sometimes returning to its original model, and sometimes departing from it." The styles of dress in this century were the same throughout Europe. We have but to look over a collection of portraits, whether of Englishmen, Frenchmen, Spaniards, or Flemings, to recognize the same features of dress, and even the same style of beard and hair in the one country that we find in the other. The portraits of the Elizabethan period, the heads of Shakespeare, Spenser, Raleigh, and Bacon, give us the costume in all its stateliness and dignity. Wherever seen, it is of Italian origin, but is most rightly characterized as Spanish, since its general adoption was a consequence of the Spanish preponderance in the world during the century. The costume, briefly described in its main points, was as follows: The lower

limbs were encased in tight hose; the trunk
hose, which met the other at the middle of

the upper leg, were puffed; the jacket, open
in front, met the trunk hose at the hips;

over this was worn a doublet, short, in the early part of the century, but in the Elizabethan time made long and close to the body, and carried down to a peak; and over all the short cloak, which Raleigh laid down in the mire that the Virgin Queen might pass over dry-shod. About the neck was the large circular ruff, that lends so much distinction to the famous heads of the time. There was almost no difference between the ruffs worn by the men and those of the women. The limited use of the word *hose*, as applied to-day, dates from the fashions of the sixteenth century. As then used, the word signified the upper slashed and puffed covering of the leg, while the name *stocking* meant the tight covering of the lower part of the leg. In time a second name, *breeches*, was applied to what had been called *hose*, and this word came to be regarded as synonymous with stockings. The head-coverings varied in form and style, from the low, flat cap worn by Henry VIII to the large-brimmed, high-crowned hat seen in most of the well-known pictures of Elizabeth's time.

The modifications of this costume, introduced by national taste and cast of mind, are entertainingly described by M. Lacroix, in the work already quoted : " In Italy, for ex- ample, dress always maintained a certain character of grandeur, ever recalling the fact that the influence of antiquity had not been altogether lost.   In Germany and Switzerland garments generally had a heavy and massive appearance, and in Holland more so.   Eng- land uniformly studied a kind of instinctive elegance and propriety.   It is a curious fact that Spain invariably partook of the heaviness peculiar to Germany, either because the Gothic element still prevailed there, or that the Walloon fashions had an especial attraction for her, owing to associations and general usage.   France was then, as she is now, fickle and capricious, fantastical and wavering, not indeed from indifference, but because she always was ready to borrow from any quarter whatever pleased her.   She never failed, at the same time, to put her own stamp on what she adopted, so as to make it essentially French, even when borrowed from Spain or Germany, Italy or England."

This lively passage is truthful, in the main,

though, perhaps, M. Lacroix would have come
nearer to the fact if, instead of describing the
German and the Spanish styles as heavy, he
had recognized them as grave. It seems to
be evident that it is rather the Spanish
gravity he is aiming at, as a complement to
the French fickleness.

Of the luxury in dress at this period there
are abundant illustrations. The Field of the
Cloth of Gold was, indeed, an occasion when
splendor and a lavish expense were in a
measure called for. The nobles in attendance
upon two young sovereigns so remarkable
for personal accomplishments as Henry the
Eighth and Francis the First must have felt
it to be a duty to display their finery, at
whatever cost; but there are many proofs
that, in more than one country, there was a
wasteful style of dress and personal expenditure which excited the anxiety of thoughtful statesmen. Sumptuary laws, so repeat-
edly proved to be powerless against the impulses of vanity and ostentation, were enacted
in every country to restrain the taste for
luxury. As in most cases of legislation on
matters properly belonging to the domain of

private authority, the laws covered too much
ground, and treated as excessive what was not
really more than unostentatious adornment.
A decree of Philip the Second, in answer to
a petition from the Cortes of Madrid, in 1563,
is worth quoting as an instance of the style
of legislation in these matters, the rather that
this king, who bears such an evil name in
history, was, in the matter of public and
private expenditure, liberal and wise to a
very uncommon degree. The edict reads:
" We ordain likewise that no one, of any
condition or quality whatever, shall wear on
his clothing, his doublet, or trunk-hose, or vest,
nor suffer to be put upon the housings or
trappings of any mule or horse, any species
of embroidery or stitched work, or ruffling,
or metal plates, or spangles, or bugling, or
plaited or twisted silk, or edgework, or
back-stitching, or threading of gold or silver,
or silk, or other material, even though the
gold and silver be false, etc."

In matters of this kind men will judge and
act for themselves, and it is but an exception
when the political authority is able to enforce
compliance with arbitrary prohibitions, like

those of Calvin in Geneva, or the Puritans in the early days of New England. The increase of wealth in a nation must show itself in the amount of thought bestowed upon costume, and the consequent elevation of the standard of refinement, for these two things act and re-act upon each other; nor is there any instance in history of a highly-refined, intellectual and cultivated people, indifferent to dress, or inclined to look upon elegance of costume as a matter to be neglected. On the contrary, it is in this form that taste begins to show itself as a people makes advances in material prosperity. It could not well be otherwise, unless the nature of man underwent a fundamental change. The social instincts assert themselves with a power proportioned to the opportunities offered for their gratification, by the ease and comfort of which men find themselves possessed. Entertainments, public and private, dinners, balls, parties of pleasure, and the like, bring people together for mutual enjoyment, and every one must seek to do honor to the occasion and to the friends he is to meet, by donning an attire that shall make him appear at his best. If civilization be anything but a name, it is certainly as natural and as instinctive in man as any of the confessedly natural appetites, since it is but the development of the instinct of selection.

Men choose what seems to them the best; and the first use of a command of means is to apply it to improving and beautifying the daily life by adding to the forms of beauty which surround it. Everything which makes objects of daily use more pleasing to the eye shows an advance toward a higher ideal of comfort and of taste; and whatever may be thought of their comparative value on the field of battle, there can be no doubt that, so far as civilization is concerned, the Sybarites were altogether higher than the Spartans. The history of England during the century under consideration bears testimony to the very great progress of the national taste in dress, so far as the employment of more costly materials is concerned. The energy and vigor with which the English entered upon their enterprises beyond the sea, and their attempts at planting colonies, their wars with Spain, which stimulated and heightened the

pride and self-confidence of the nation, and
the activity of their commerce, were not more
remarkable than the sudden intellectual and
artistic flowering of their genius. They displayed their power in every field of activity;
and their domestic economy, which had so recently disgusted the cultivated taste of Erasmus, began to wear that attractive look of
cleanliness and repose which it has never since
resigned.

The floors were no longer covered with the
foul rushes that concealed the bones and
scraps, but were spread with rich and beautiful carpets; the windows were carefully
glazed, and the rooms were furnished with
the finest tables and chairs, made of the rare
woods brought from beyond the sea. The
presence of books and works of art, in
many a home of the middle class, showed an
appreciation of the best results of civilization
not common in similar dwellings on the Continent; and the inmates of these houses were
clad in garments every way suited, for richness of material and artistic fitness, to their
surroundings. It would be an error to suppose that the upward movement in these im-

portant matters was confined to the highest classes. The whole nation was advancing with an equal front, and there has probably been no period in English history at which the general condition of the people was, on the whole, so fairly prosperous. We may look back upon the Sixteenth Century as the time when the decisively progressive movement toward a simplified ideal of manly costume began in England, which has ever since that period held the foremost place as the arbiter of taste in this matter.

CHAPTER V.

THE most marked feature in the perfection in the highest forms of American dressing, as applied to the man, is the emphatic influence of English styles and conceits running through every branch of the wardrobe, whether for lounging costume, street attire, or the more carefully designed garments for dress occasions. Yet, strongly pronounced as this influence is, the fashions that reign in America are undoubtedly conglomerate; that is, while partaking in all of the individual characteristics of the methods and traditions of Albion, they unite many subordinate features from the varying nationalities peopling our shores—thus giving a distinctively new cut and trimming to the garment, which marks its wearer, wherever found over the world. This American tendency, while following no immutable law, is very largely governed by climate, and by the rapid, exciting, bustling life led on the Western Continent.

In all matters of dress, as between the United States and Great Britain, one prominent fact stands out—English heaviness and American lightness, and the appearance of both when the reality does not exist. Take the average Englishman—his staunch frame, ample feet, healthy contour, and high color—and you will perceive a solidity in the make-up of his clothes, a sense of the durable, the non-tearable, a feeling of utility throughout, in which artistic lines and decorative work are entirely secondary. You are sure a rainstorm or a good ducking would not send him post-haste to his tailor with a new order. He is dressed upon lines that defy the elements, and he is not afraid, however he walks, sits, or reposes, or whatever his physical action, that he will fall to pieces like the harlequin in the play. His boots have broad and substantial heels and are of heavy calfskin, or otherwise, as the case may be, and are designed for longevity, not beauty, while the hat follows the same general law. Now note the American moving in a parallel cir-

cle at home, and who is not afflicted with
that form of Anglomania which causes him
to follow English styles, purely in the vein
of abject and ignorant imitation, and you will
find him physically a lighter man, smaller
boned, wirier, with a certain swiftness of
walk, a hurried, nervous manner—a being, in
fine, suited to this bracing atmosphere, and
conscious that dress is a powerful social
factor in America, an almost free passport to
a general acquaintanceship at sight, if he can
bear out his title to respectability and good
address. With him we find a boot made for
the foot's shape, a considerable heel, and a
laborious quality of instep-architecture which
tells the story that he is a rider in chaises
and not a walker. Then his silk hat is almost one-half as light as that of his English
cousin, while every suggestion of his garments
is that the ornamental dominates the useful. The snug fit, the lighter quality of fabric, the absence of lounging ease, and the
ever-buttoned coat to the regulation form,
just suits the national temperament, as we
watch our well-dressed American on his
saunter—no, walk—up Fifth avenue; for

Englishmen saunter, and Americans, arrow-straight, are conscious of eye-fascinations created by the outer man.

The distinctions we here make cannot be offensive to either nationality, for they are true from whatever point of view, and are demonstrated in whatever we find in the fine or mechanic arts of the two countries. For example: England, in her monuments, statuary, paintings, and architecture, formulates the idea of the bold and massive; something for time and wear; something that will keep long alive this period of her history, as creations of former epochs delight and instruct this age to-day. Her buildings are sunk in deep foundations, and the permanent granite blocks, which rise in simple forms, tell the story that remote ages will find them as perfect as when first they rose against the sky. All of the outward and visible life of that people partake of the same characteristics —in their carriages, locomotives, household furniture, and even with journals and reviews and periodicals we note the same idea of permanency. It is thus that a man who finds his daily walk in Fleet street, and not in

Broadway, is filled with the ever-pervading feeling of the enduring, of moving in a world that is not of yesterday, to-day, and to-morrow alone, and amid surroundings where a foothold has been made that will remain until all things perishable shall merge into the common ruin! Were London a city of internal revolutions, subject to the devastations of armed mobs, like Paris, and given over under fitful dynasties to great building fevers, to the tearing down and reconstructing on modern lines, as Baron Haussmann did to Paris, the French capital, under the Third Empire, it is possible that outward London, taking on a new stony garb, might change the habitual thought of the English people, as we have observed in some of the larger Continental capitals within the present generation. It is true that there has been some vandalism of recent date in the sweeping away of ancient historic landmarks like Temple Bar, but they are hardly worthy of notice in this great city of the world now housing nearly 5,000,000 of people.

How different all this to the changes in

New York, even in a decade! Rushing from
one school of architecture to another, building thirteen stories in the air, having a châ-
teau from the Loire, a palace from Unter den
Linden, a castle from Warwickshire, a cha-
let from Lake Como, Moorish façades from
Andalusia, and Kiosque forms from the
Orient—what modern whim from the arts will
not the American embrace? And, following
out this inquiry to its legitimate conclusion,
do we not find a disposition to draw from
parallel fountains of perfection in other arts,
and notably in the art of dressing? Do we
not find the American making a composite
fashion, coming from all peoples, which, as
generations roll by, must become the dominant
one among men? Can it be supposed, moreover, that, in the great dress reform movement that must ultimately sweep over the
world, America, stripped of its provincialism,
and susceptible to influence from whatever
clime and people, will not be the most fitting
and impressionable nation to lead the van?
Let us, in the light of these facts and queries,
mark the general influence, in fact an absolute and easily measurable one, which Eng-

land has had on these United States during
those years since the civil war. Primarily,
all that there is in this art of dressing in the
United Kingdom proceeds from London. It
is in the Metropolis that the tailor starts
his propaganda which reaches from John
O'Groat's to Land's End, and ultimately
through the clubs, travelers, diplomatic corps,
and pioneer cutters, as far as the Asiatic
possessions of the Czar; for it is incontro-
vertible that, in the present age of cylindrical
wear, so to speak, the fashions are made by
the London artist. There is a popular delusion that the Court, and particularly the
Prince of Wales, has only to appear in a garment, however grotesque in pattern, and all
clubland will speedily follow. This, however, is not so, although the crown circles have
a reasonable and a legitimate influence over
the male wardrobe; but, when the Prince
and his coteries, some years ago, essayed to
proclaim anew the era of blue coats and brass
buttons, the up-start craze died in its own
incubation. Mighty as may be the fiat of this
lofty personage, and mysterious the charms
of the recognized social autocrat of the dy-

nasty, English gentlemen would not retrograde in dress, even in the face of such a
mandate, and the brazen suit lay fallow and
died. It had a brief life in New York and
other American cities, and the genial Sam
Ward, even up to his latest moments, never
appeared in any other garb than the doomed
evening wear of less than a score of years
ago.

CHAPTER VI.

WHO, it may be asked, are arbiters of style, going away down to the very foundations? With the fair sex, it is easy enough to answer. It may be an Empress, with every resource of historic inventive art to aid a naturally gifted mind and eye, a refined sense of the beautiful, and a splendid conception of and feeling for color, and with an abundant purse to carry out the day-dreams of a poetic temperament—those visions of gown, bonnet, and slipper, at the Tuileries, Compiègne, Fontainebleau, and Longchamps. So it may be a hapless Camille, the story of whose wondrous life fills one of the most pathetic and thrilling places on the modern stage; a Bernhardt with her gloves, a Langtry with her hose, and a Judic with her corsage low. Herein are the celebrities tyrants as absolute as Shahs, and the dress-makers and milliners slaves in a bondage as abject as the former-time serf of the Czar. The distribution of fashion's prerogatives, since the ex-Empress Eugenie ceased to reign, however, has been among competent leaders, although that imperial lady was the greatest of her time. Casting our eyes backward, we find no such potent figure in the feminine kingdom since light-hearted Marie-Antoinette reigned over the coiffures, the drapery, and the foot-wear of fashionable Europe; and when those two great lights went out forever—one on the guillotine in the Palace de la Révolution, and the other in the agony of widowhood at Chiselhurst, to be closely followed by the death of her own boy-prince —there came that dispersion of styles rendered emphatic by the leadership of women made conspicuous in other ways. But men, at least in civil life, are not thus led. It is in London that we probe this query to the ultimate source; for no instructed mind in this age will deny that in male attire the idea and general outline, however modified subsequently, proceed from the brains and experience of the artist-tailor of that metropolis. Let us say, too, that some superfine

people may be disposed to sneer at the word
artist-tailor. Why should they? Here we

have our sculptor, setting about to make a
shapely human figure What does he do?

He masses the requisite quantity of clay, and with his hands fashions it into rough proportions, and then, with calipers, dividers, and other measuring instruments, he works to the exactness of outline required by the sketch-form which he copies. It is the eye and the yard-stick, after all; and it is no more, no less, with the tailor. Likewise should it be known that no eminent sculptor ever considers a draped figure perfect, or ready for critical inspection, before he calls in a quick-eyed and experienced craftsman from the cutter's board. A further fact is, that a cutter of exceptional gifts and standing can earn more money, at wage, than the average sculptor, all over the world. He must needs know the imperfections of one's physique almost at a glance, without letting their unhappy possessor be aware of his intelligent scrutiny; he must plot out in his mind the best method to cover them up. While preserving the conventional lines and seams of the prevailing fashion, he must, to be explicit, make out of an awkwardly put together man, who has a slatternly gait and a jointless carriage, a fair imitation of the true Adonis, without hurting his patron's feelings. Look at that man yonder!—the scion of an ancient Manhattan house—with an income beyond the dream of want, an unconquerable ambition to be thought handsome in form, careful in dress, and, withal, irresistible at the shrine of Venus. He is not ill-looking, you proclaim, with your masculine dictum; and the ladies along the avenue, they say : " Isn't he too lovely for anything?" Yet, simple mortals! that is not a God-made man you see; it is a tailor-made man. Invade the sanctity of his chamber when the curfew tolls the knell of parting day, and the mysteries of this alert divinity stand revealed before you. Shall the picture be etched—the limbs, the chest, the shoulders and their knifey blades? Nay! There lie the secrets of the shop!

The absolute fixedness of the tradition that an English gentleman must have his own private tailor prohibits him from patronizing the great establishments that sell readymade wear. No untoward financial outlook will cause a well-dressed Briton to sway from this habit of a life-time. The curious feature of it is, too, that he always adheres to the same shop which has, perhaps, been patronized for generations by his family. Reasons in abundance exist for this loyalty to the same house; but, as will be obvious, it is often a mistaken course, for the craftsmanship changes, as do the directors and manner of doing business. Still, there is a social flavor given to the man, who cannot obtain it otherwise, by mentioning, in a careless manner, that he had left an order at Poole's. It is well known to all worldly men that this deceased autocrat exercised a dominion in England of no mean dimensions. Furnishing the funds to Louis Napoleon to maintain his quasi-dignity as an Imperial prince in exile, he had more to do in bringing about the early days of the French Empire than many dream. This, and the patronage of the Crown, the herding of the nobility to his shop in Sackville street, gave him at least an assumed importance which made the exotic man marvel. This was, all queer on any reasonable grounds, illustrated thus: An American gentleman of commanding physique entered his shop one morning and said:

"I wish to get measured for some clothes. I am in a hurry."

"Your introduction, if you please!" said the trim manager, with a bow quite at right-angles with the perpendicular.

The American eyed him contemptuously, and with a gesture of impatience, drawing forth his morocco envelope, he exhibited a roll of £50 Bank of England notes, saying:

"Here are my letters of introduction."

"They will not go here, sir!" replied he decisively, when the would-be customer exhibited his card as the accredited United States Consul-General to an Oriental capital. He demurred again, and the disgusted diplomat, with a choice volley of accentuated allusions to sheol and its viceroy, departed.

This custom of the house alluded to, widespread as it is, and now employed among the best merchant tailors of New York, is not snobbery, as it would naturally appear on the surface and to the unthinking. To be plain, it is simply wise mercantile precaution, as the author has tested many times in New York, London, and Paris. A high class of business could not be done without a safeguard like this. To illustrate, an unknown gentleman enters a shop and gives a cash order for a suit of clothes, without revealing his identity or pecuniary responsibility. They are made and paid for. Subsequently he goes again, and obtains a second suit under the same circumstances. After a time he orders several hundred dollars worth of clothes, with orders to send them to his address. They are made, and despatched "Collect on delivery," but the customer pleads for time, or is indignant. In this case it is, perhaps, policy to mollify him and extend the credit, running the risk of eventual payment rather than have the garments thrown back on the maker's hands, because then he could not dispose of them at one-quarter their charged value. Thus it will be readily seen that a merchant selling only the higher class of articles, and dealing with gentlemen, and those of responsibility, wishes to know for whom he is making clothes. It is more important to him than ready cash sales to those who consider steady patronage as an implied favor to the tailor, who must in return extend, from pure gratitude, hazardous credit for large amounts.

When English reign in dress began to be felt in America, shortly before the close of the civil war, the male costume on this side of the water presented some curious incongruities. The author found himself one among several Englishmen only who had come to New York for permanence. The field seemed large, the growth of a better taste rapid, and a wish, where there was a way, to use only the best fabrics to adorn the body. The outlook was, moreover, very enticing from another standpoint: The Americans were willing to pay high prices, and consequently every device known to the tailor's skill and invention was brought into requisition to make elegant and attractive clothes, some of which exist to-day, while the others have gone out, let us hope, forever. Then came the period of the built-out shoulders and padded chest, which gave to a consumptive sapling the appearance of a diminished Hercules, whose spring-bottom trousers were borrowed from the aquatic fevers which were then the expensive tastes of the wealthier. White duck suits and cream-colored wear, both of which have a

history, were spasms of the era, and traces of
them may yet be seen among those who have
been reduced to the last stitch of a once
opulent wardrobe. But however these facts,
those of the English method in New York
soon found that it was on the cards to make
the gentlemen of this city the best dressed in
the world ; and so they are, beyond all question, to-day. They pay for, demand, and get,
the finest skill in cutting, the best workmanship, trimmings of the rarest quality, and
only such clothes as are used at the highest
courts of Europe. And this has been one result of English influence on American dress.

CHAPTER VII.

CYLINDRICAL CLOTHES.

It is a matter of great difficulty to assign a certain date to the origin of the cylindrical garment which we call *trousers*, for the farther back we push our researches into the history of wearing apparel, the more are we made to see that some dawning of the shape has flitted before the eyes of men, at times, in every land under the sun. Again and again it appears as if the Egyptians, the Assyrians, the Babylonians, were on the point of seizing finally the great idea, and giving to it a permanent form as a constituent part of their national costume. But the history of this great discovery was not to be added to the long roll of the conquests of Rameses or Assurbanipal. The captives that stand stripped and huddled together before the great king, on the walls of the temples and on the alabaster slabs, seem, indeed, at times to wear, for their only covering, what suggests the future distinctive and typical portion of the costume of civilized man; but it is only a suggestion, and passes as it came.

It is not in the Nile, nor in Mesopotamia, that we find the genesis of this article. Ancient Persia possessed the form, and succeeded, when under Sapor she divided with Rome the supremacy of the world, in imposing it upon the haughty empire. How far the invention of the cylinder belonged to Persia is, however, matter of doubt, and it seems probable that the garment was rather an inheritance from the prehistoric Aryans, than a discovery wrought out by a later thinker in an organized Oriental society, where the accepted ideal of manly attire was the long tunic or robe with its flowing lines. This extreme antiquity seems the more likely, that we find the far western kinsmen of the ancient Persians, the Germans and the Gauls, equally in possession of this significant shape, at a period when history barely knows their names, and records them as those of barbarous and untamable tribes. The captives represented on the column of Trajan wear trousers; and the true Anglo-Saxon word *breeches* is but an English form of the Irish and Gaelic name for the Gaulish garment.

The Chinese undoubtedly invented their own breeches; but it would be a mistake to attribute to them the communication of the idea to the West, for China has never entered into the general movement of the world's history until in recent days, and forms almost literally a world by itself, as much isolated from the rest of the globe as if it were part of another planet.

We are forced back upon the conclusion that the inventor of this part of dress is, like the inventor of the alphabet, or the discoverer of the plough, absolutely beyond the reach of the inquirer. His work speaks for him, or, at least, it lives and moves for him, wearing always, under whatever imperfect shape a bungling artist may have given it, some portion of a likeness to the finished beauty of outline which floated only before the imagination of the mind that conceived it, to become a palpable reality only when the fulness of time had brought, with advancing science and more fully developed resources, the artistic intelligence and culture needed to fix the idea forever.

It is only the first step that is difficult, says the proverb. This applies to all inventions as to every form of labor; but it is equally true, that no discovery is perfect in the shape first given to it. To see the fitness of means to ends, is in itself an intellectual step that implies activity and nimbleness of mind; but there is hardly less activity called for in the amplification of a simple idea to make it stand by its own strength. It was a great thing to have seen that man, himself a collection of pipes and cylinders enclosed in an outer cylinder, might best be attired in cylindrical garments, and one cannot but be struck by the wonderful instinct of genius in the unknown inventor of the trousers, who sprang forward mentally, so to speak, across the gap of centuries, to create, when society could hardly be said to have an organization, a form at once typical of and indispensable to the most complex and elaborate civilization. "Measure a great period," says Emerson, "by the comparative lack of elevation of any one man above the rest."

How towering, measured by this rule, is the height of the unknown genius we are considering! He put forth his idea, and not to wholly inattentive minds, for it was adopted and made familiar; but the ages slowly rolled away, and there came no second intellect to develop and modify the first rude form. Men were contented with the cylinder of cloth, or linen, or cotton, or skins, provided only it covered the leg and was fastened about the ankle. Grace, fitness, delicate adaptation to the peculiarities of the wearer, no one of these things could come to the thought of the earlier followers of the great discoverer. What was done seemed to them sufficient, and they went on fabricating and wearing their breeks, or breeches, or trousers, through the long ages of monotonous style, until the artist, the thinker in cloth, was found. It is noticeable how little the artists, of a day even so late as that of Holbein, seem to care for the possibilities of nobleness that lie in the undeveloped breeches. A study of the illustrations made by this great master on the margin of his copy of the *Encomium Moriæ* of Erasmus shows how

entirely he missed the wonderfully suggestive future in the shape of this garment.
All through the Middle Ages we find the
same inadequate treatment of the nether
covering.

That most popular story of the time, the
"Adventures and Jests of Tyll Owlglass"
(Eulenspiegel), certainly not less popular
than the *Reineke Fuchs*, presents the trousers
always in the burlesque and ridiculous manner which betrays in a folk-book the popular
conception of the subject. It might be
thought that this point of view was natural
in the less enlightened times of the thirteenth
and fourteenth centuries, and in the backward North; but what is to be said of
Rabelais, great genius and profound scholar
as he was? Surely, even his royal license,
as lord of the springs of wise and thoughtful
mirth, had taken too little note of the serious
element in the history and unfolding of the
great subject. For, after all, what is more
suggestive of manly dignity and power, what
more indispensable to an impressive and
kingly bearing before the world, than legs
sufficiently attired and equal to the support

of the chest—the house of courage, and the head—the dome of intelligence and reflection?

BUILT OUT SHOULDERS AND SPRING BOTTOMS.

CHAPTER VIII.

THE TRUE ARTIST-TAILOR.

SEVENTY passages across the Atlantic Ocean, and always connected with the subject matter of this book, have taught the author that on either side of the great pond there are those who fashion the clothes of men in a conscientious and honorable spirit, not less earnest and painstaking than the labor of the painter or sculptor in his effort to please the eye. But the designer of wear has an additional task, not imposed on him who deals in clay or pigments. With beauty he is bound to combine comfort and durability, with the vexatious knowledge that his skill must soon disappear by the attrition of constant action and the inevitable decay of the fabric. Is it not fair, then, to place the accomplished tailor, deeply instructed in the mysteries of his craft, in close proximity to the sculptor, who follows conventional forms and fashions inelastic figures? We think all will concede that it requires no mean perceptive powers to follow all of the sinuous curves of the human body, fill out their defects, give an easy setting to the apparel, and supply a wanted *chic* to the pose of the man himself. Yet such is the office of the cutter in any first-class house of this day; and right royally is he paid, too, often as high as $5,000 a year, considerably in excess of the salary of the President of Yale College and the highest professors in other celebrated institutions of learning here and abroad.

Tailors, therefore, who prove their attainments, command an exclusive and wealthy patronage, particularly in New York, where the liberality of patrons permits the maker to secure only the finest workmanship. Time was when waistcoats were provided with cotton backs, but now these will not do, and silk has taken the place. This and other innovations constantly appear, in order to maintain the high standard compelled by high prices. But there is a limit to the embellishment of a true gentleman's wear; for, while elegance is sought, the limit must be drawn at the tasteful outline of fashion without extremes, never descending to the odd or *bizarre,* or suggesting that most odious of all spectacles in cloth—vulgar ostentation. Here it might be well to ask, "Who is a well-dressed man?" Is he that flamboyant biped with blazing scarf, patent-leather shoes, and glittering jewelry, swaggering up Fifth Avenue beside a comely dame, his nostrils dilating with surcharged pride, attacking the harmless atmosphere with his gold-headed stick while meandering through the gaping pedestrians on a Sunday afternoon? Witness his make-up, for his fair companion is close at his elbow, with a smile of sweet contentment and a facial notification to her sister promenaders, as much as to say, in plain English, "Match him for a gentleman if you can!" Scrutinize him closely. You observe that his hat is exaggerated in form, the pomade glistens on his hair and whiskers like the sheen on polished porphyry; his shoulders, built out, give him a breadth of beam requiring a swath through the crowd ample for two of his natural kind; his waist is drawn in by corsets, his legs to the ankles are shaped like inverted cones, while the shoes, with their heels close to the ball of the foot, cause this work of art to amble along with visible pain and difficulty. **Now, is** this man dressed like a gentleman, **for one of** birth he will **show** you he is, by **the** mention **of** his family, and **by the exhibition of his parchments?** Un-happily, such a figure, **not over-drawn** either, **has often been** seen on our thoroughfares, at **the** opera, and in fashionable assemblies, and the ladies think him an artist in his attire, one bold enough to consult the arts, and alto-gether **too** beautiful **to** behold. It is a fact, also, that **many ladies of the** highest circles, and despising **the** effeminate **man,** would court this *outré* creature **rather** than **one** of **quiet** apparel. Herein, **for** effect **on the** other **sex,** men who adhere to the characteristic modesty of the true gentleman in attire are at **a** considerable disadvantage; **for,** *as women dress for women, men aress for men and women.* Only the affected and the eccentric **go to** the length **of the** curiosity **just** de-scribed.

Therefore, **the** assumption must **be** plain to **the** reader, that the well-dressed man is one **whose** garments, ornaments, and head and **foot wear, are** such that he would not attract general attention by any staggering peculiarity of his garb. Herein is the true secret of the art of dressing, and he who has not yet learned this lesson is several grades down in social culture.

By attracting attention to one's clothes, it is not meant to be understood that a well-dressed man is not noticeable, for most assuredly he is, to the cultivated and artistic eye, and to every tailor who knows his business. Even when the cloth be not fine in quality, the cut and set of his apparel will be the striking feature at once. Hence let it be said that simplicity, without display, in all the varied costumes, those for morning, walking, evening, full dress, riding, hunting, and yachting, should be the feeling throughout. You must say, "he is perfectly dressed," without exactly knowing the reason why,—whatever his physical deformities or attenuations. How often do we see, in mixed assemblies, for instance, a gifted and brilliant fellow, through whose wretchedly cut suit the experienced eye of the tailor can detect an almost perfect form, true to the lines of the Apollo Belvidere, and yet there he is, misshapen, ugly in outline, shrunken here and bulging there, all due to machine-made clothes. Yonder in the porch is another. How the ladies admire his *svelte* figure, his graceful carriage and showy build. And yet, place these two men side by side, nude, and what the contrast in the flesh!—the God-made man and the tailor-made man. But when the former can be appropriately dressed, we then indeed have perfection. Such an instance is the pride of every true artist in cloth, for, if he be true to his art, he will not countenance its degradation; he will not, to please a patron, make sloppy or grotesque garments; nor will he permit to go forth from his shop any article of wear which will injure his professional standing.

CHAPTER IX.

ELEVATED STANDARD OF TASTE AND WORK-MANSHIP.

The author could name hundreds of cases within his own experience where he has been forced to decline to execute orders for ridiculous patterns of wear from patrons of celebrity, on two continents, simply because he would not consent to debase an art only perfected after years of careful workmanship and zealous study and observation; and it should here be laid down as an inflexible law, by every honest tailor, that no patron should be allowed to depart with a suit of ill-fitting clothes, under any circumstances. This is a duty which is owing, not only to the customer, but to the craft itself; and it matters not what may be the conceit of the patron, the outside world is certain to credit the garment as worn by an ass and fabricated by a fool. Nor should pecuniary gain for a moment hamper, or in any way influence the mind of, the maker and designer, for such mistaken acquisitiveness, in the long run, is a losing game.

In laying down this principle to those young in the business, and who are ambitious, not only of gain, but of repute for high artistic excellence, it is well to observe that the production of finished clothing to man's measure involves a keen eye, a large constructive and inventive faculty, and a general following of prevailing styles. There is a satisfaction greater than the compensating dollars, to the cutter and fitter who can point out a well-dressed man on the avenue, and say, " That is my work!"

When Americans first began to perceive that the fashions came from London, it was odd to observe a man order and pay for a hundred dollar suit of clothes, and have the rest of his wear, for example, about the neck, of the crudest kind. It was the habit of one of the first of the old-time fashionable tailors of New York to keep on hand a supply of collars and neckties and scarfs to place on customers who came to be measured for a new suit of clothes. He was inflexible about this,

and lost many orders by his despotic mandate. But now this has nearly all passed
away, and the American begins to have a
wardrobe something on the same scale as the
Englishman of quality. It may be taken as
a fact, however, that where the American
buys six suits a year the Englishman buys
twelve. Take the average London club-man,
with or without title, and he delights in ac-
cumulating vast quantities of clothes adapted
to special uses and varying occasions. His
array of boots, hats, bags, canes, and um-
brellas, would fit out a respectable shop. This
comes from the ability and habit to have a
valet—a personage who is not very popular
as yet with the young and able-bodied American. Perhaps this may be because our leisure class is very limited as yet, and furthermore, when one finds himself the fortunate
possessor of inherited wealth, instead of giving himself entirely over to the varieties of
dress, he proceeds to expend the major portion of his time in multiplying his already
ample dollars. Still, the rich youth of New
York and other American cities are the class
depended on by the first-class tailors to sup-

port high style and to give liberal orders, keeping closely up with the more advanced movements in the old world. Were tailors left dependent on those past middle life or in declining age, the Americans would be a poorly attired people. There seems to be a gravitation toward carelessness in this respect as the average American grows older, and even as he grows richer. That there is a somewhat fine philosophy drawn here is doubtless true, for the opulent citizen may be prone to mentally asseverate "I can afford to dress as I please; I will despise the pomps of the day." Such, perchance, was the argument of the late A. T. Stewart, who used to sit in his office, at Broadway and Chambers streets, in a well-worn suit of rusty broadcloth, without the sign of jewel or ornament of any kind, while his humblest clerk would be radiant and spruce in such wear that it was evident he had to stint his stomach to adorn his back. The true-artist tailor cannot but look upon examples of the kind of the celebrated merchant prince as exceedingly pernicious, and as nothing more nor less than an exceedingly narrow sham. Here was Mr. Stewart, who was a magnificent patron of art, who proclaimed his nice and discriminating taste by purchasing all the richest stuffs from all of the markets of the world—a dealer whose stock was thousands of times richer and more varied than the magnificent goods which went to the Venetian market in the palmy days of the mediæval carnivals; and yet he played the part of austerity in personal dress—a part quite as wearisome as great care and thought over the daily costume.

CHAPTER X.

Leaving a type of men of whom Mr. Stewart was a forcible example, it is well to let professions and public officials of the country pass in review.

On all sides it must be admitted that to a professional man, be he lawyer, editor, author, doctor, minister, artist, sculptor, or librarian, fine address, and consequently fine dress, is of the supremest importance. Not that foppery is to be tolerated, but apparel of the first quality would not only augment his income, add to his personal dignity, but would tell wonderfully with the ladies, who have so much to do with shaping his career. There is a certain class of professional men who think all that is necessary is cleanliness, and that too much attention to the outer man betrays a mental weakness which might influence those concerned in making his reputation to believe that such might be the main purpose of his existence. Yet the

successful practitioners of the law and medi-
cine have seen that no small measure of their
triumphs has come by being presentable—
that is, by so following the styles that there
could be no suggestion of shabbiness on the
one hand, or loudness on the other. While
all of the professions sin mightily against the
laws of dress at this moment, still within a
very few years there has been a very rapid
advance for the better. Take the literary
guild as an example. Years ago a writer of
power and attainments was a slouchy individual with unkempt hair, soiled garments,
and rusty externals generally. Now and
then we found an exception, as in the late
N. P. Willis, but the exceptions were not
many. Since that period the multiplication
of clubs, the movement to and fro across the
sea, and the increased income to be derived
by literary toil, and the actual founding of
an American school of literature, have all
contributed to make the author, pamphleteer,
and journalist, a sightlier figure, to be further improved in outward aspect, let us hope,
as time rolls on. Nor should we deny to the
far-reaching and powerful stage its just meed

of recognition, in the perpetual and intelligent stimulus it has lent to the spread of the
fine art of dressing among men and women.
The hero, the walking gentleman, and the
refined villain cast in the noisome surroundings of squalor, poverty, and crime, have an
excellent chance to exhibit all of the fine
points of dressing; and, executed as these
costumes are, with infinite pains, and reaching
every branch of the wardrobe of a gentleman, the impression made on the beholder is
strengthened by the dramatic action, the
memorable situations and plot, and the power
of the piece itself. It is not contended that
the walking gentleman of the stage is an appropriate copy for the street or drawing-
room, owing to the inevitable heightening of
effects before the foot-lights; still, the artistic
feeling and display are before the eye, and
have had no inconsiderable directing force in
teaching mankind to dress better.

From what has been said, we think it not
too much to add that it is the duty of every
true artist-tailor, as circumstances permit, to
instill into the minds of the gentlemen of the
professions the absolute necessity of superi-

ority over others in the daily raiment. In the first place, their contact with others is frequent, and they reach all classes of life, from the lowest to the highest; and, being born of intellectual aspect, they are more suitable for artistic dressing than those whose faces have become stolid in pursuit of gain. If it were appreciated by them that a man suitably attired is really a delightful spectacle to the eye, we fancy there would be a greater readiness to look out for the person. But it may be pleaded that professional men cannot afford these luxuries; their incomes are limited and their general expenses high. This is a fallacious kind of reasoning. The man who pays sixty or seventy dollars for a suit of perfectly-fitting clothes is practicing a more intelligent economy than he who purchases at one-third the sum, to say nothing of the pleasure of wearing he enjoys in the interval. The durability, also, is in the better articles, as well as the pattern and attractive outline.

In the official life of America, and by that is meant, of course, those who occupy the offices, and their immediate beneficiaries, there is given an opportunity to influence the national dress not to be ignored, and particularly since the dawn of civil service reform. But if we pass by the subordinates and come to those of dignified station, we do not find a very pleasing prospect. Beginning at the top round, the United States has had but one well-dressed President since the administration of James Buchanan; and he—President Arthur. There can certainly be no earthly excuse for the Chief Magistrate, with his body attendant close at hand, not to set an example of gentlemanly and becoming garb to the whole nation. Likewise with both houses of Congress. They represent in their number the many communities by whom they are delegated to make laws, and their example in Washington, wont to claim its architecture as the most imposing and splendid of modern times, would go far to leaven the masses. Again, there is a habit among the American people, with their fresh civilization, that should be rooted out from the national customs. In all communities, and among all classes, the people think it incumbent to wear only their best clothes on Sundays and festival occasions. We take it there could be nothing more vulgar than this —basing this statement on every-day common sense principles. Why, let us ask, should a man be better dressed on Sundays than on any other day? Be he a business man, he has his suit for the counting-room; for evening calls, his frock-coat or dress-suit; and the various other forms of garments suitable for specific occasions. We can readily understand why mechanics, and those doing severe manual labor, should preserve a portion of their wardrobe for the set-apart days; but, for one able to afford the outlay, the man should be no better dressed one day than another, and at all times well.

Those who follow the rule of uniform good dressing form a very large class at present in America, and they are more independent than the gentry of England and the Continent in their choice of tailors. If the cut and fit of their orders are not approved they seek a new shop, and are thus handed around among the upper houses, whereas in England the patron seldom changes, but is satisfied with what is meted out to him.

CHAPTER XI.

It is interesting to note the derivation of the name by which this portion of dress is known at the present day. The word *trousers* is not an old form. Mr. Skeat remarks that, in older books, this word is found without the latter *r*, as *troozes*, *trouzes*, and even *trooze*, like the Lowland Scotch *trews;* and in Henry V, iii, 7, 57, Shakespeare has the corrupt form *strossers*. The word is said to have been particularly used of the nether garments of the Irish, and Mr. Skeat gives, with others, a quotation from Sir T. Herbert's Travels, as follows: "Their breeches, like the Irish *trooze*, have hose and stockings sewed together."

In Ford's Perkin Warbeck, iii, 2, the stage direction reads: "Four wild Irish in trowses."

The original of the word is, undoubtedly, the French *trousses*, trunk-hose or breeches, but at first, and in the singular, a bundle or case, such as a quiver for arrows, as given in

Cotgrave's dictionary, quoted by Mr. Skeat. The limited meaning of trunk-hose, or of that portion of the body more directly concerned with that form of garment, is the one preserved in the French familiar idiom quoted by Carlyle in his *Frederick the Great*, in his account of the unfortunate Russian lady whose physical infirmities compelled her to travel " *Toujours un lavement à ses trousses.*" The mutations and chances which have overtaken this word are, perhaps, not more surprising than those which most words are made to undergo; but it gives us a moment's pause to find the accepted English name to have been, but two hundred years ago, applied only to the dress of the wild Irish. No Englishman of to-day would use the general American name of *pantaloons* for this indispensable and inexpressible article. One must say trousers; but when he says it he makes use of a word French by origin, Irish by naturalization, and English by adoption only from the Irish. It must be expected that this word will continually gain ground in the United States, since it has in its favor the influence of English example and social prestige ; and if it were only that the form of it precludes its being abbreviated, like its competitor, in a shape—

Hateful, horrible, monstrous, not to be told,

this were enough to make every one pray for its speedy and permanent triumph.

The preferred American name of *panta-loons* is important enough to claim a few words taken from Mr. Skeat's dictionary. The word is there explained as of Greek origin, through the Italian, and is said to be a personal name, meaning *all-lion*, from *panta*, wholly, and *león*, lion. Littré, the great French lexicographer, gives a different derivation and meaning—*all-pitiful;* also from the Greek. The former explanation seems the better, though one does not like to question a positive statement by Littré. In Italy the name is peculiarly Venetian, and the people of that city are known to the other Italians as *Pantaloons*, just as Londoners are called Cockneys. In the Italian comedy the *pantalone* is a covetous and amorous old dotard, who is made the butt of the piece. Mahn says that St. Pantaleone

is the patron saint of Venice, and that his
name is a very common baptismal name in
that city.   There is a St. Pantaleone, whose
day is July 27; but it is a little odd that
neither Herr Mahn nor Mr. Skeat seems to
have remembered that, if Venice has a patron
saint, it is St. Mark.   Lord Byron's etymology of the name Pantaloon is justly described by Mr. Skeat as extraordinary and
even ridiculous; and it is well to call attention to this point, because for one person
who looks into an etymological dictionary
there are, happily, five hundred who read
Byron; and, of these, many never think of
questioning his authority.   It is the preroga-
tive of a genius so splendid to subdue and
to dazzle the reader; but all ought to know
that in questions of learning Byron is ruled
out of court.   Whatever the etymology of
the word, it came from Venice, and was in
time transferred from the men who were
known as Pantaloons to the kind of breeches
which they wore.   It is instructive to observe that, while the English have adopted
a name of French origin, the French recognize only the Italian name of the inex-

pressibles; though it does not appear by what secret sympathies men are guided in their selection of such terms. The fact is such, and beyond this no one appears to be able to penetrate; for each nation has possessed, in ordinary usage, the word it now seems to have finally discarded. The pantaloons were worn under that name in the time of the Restoration. In an inventory of apparel provided for Charles II, in 1679, we find a complete suit of one material under the familiar designation of coat, waistcoat, and breeches. Pantaloons are mentioned in the same inventory, and a yard and a half of lutestring allowed for them.* These pantaloons were loose in the upper part, and puffed, fitting closer on the lower leg, and terminating in stockings. There is evidence in Hudibras that the garment had been adopted, not directly from Italy, but from France. In Part I, Canto 3, occur these lines:

> And as the French we conquered once,
> Now give us laws for pantaloons.

The evidence is not conclusive, since the

---

* Planché, History of British Costume, p. 327.

French fashion might have come in to modify the style of garments already in use;
but the lines admit of the other interpreta-
tion. It is probable that the struggle between the two names in the American world
will end, not, as some might wish, in the
definite triumph of one form to the exclusion of the other, but in a kind of compro-
mise which will give to the form *trousers*
"*les grandes et les petites entrées*" in good
society, and leave to the other the ever wide
domain of the great multitude which, for
fear of some more vigilant guardians of the
democratic idea, we hesitate to designate as
the masses. Not that the term has in it anything necessarily offensive, since it is a self-
evident proposition that, when the population of the world amounts, according to
Behm and Wagner, the best of all authorities,
to something over 1,400,000,000, it is a mere
statement of scientific fact to speak of the
masses of mankind. We may call them what
we will, masses they will remain, because
they will always largely outnumber those
who aim at a high and refined ideal of culture and civilization in thought, and in the

outward expression of thought as manifested in language, manners, and attire. Man has always, until he has caught the divine fire, what Swift has called an alacrity in sinking.

One has but to give a glance at what we call our monuments, in the shape of columns and of statues, to recognize the downward gravitation of the average man; and the one saying which preserves King Bomba's memory from entire detestation is his witty remark on the proposed remodeling of the uniform of his soldiers, mere mercenaries of a tyrant who thought as basely of his people as of himself, and dreaded nothing so much as the wakening of individual manhood and the feeling of national pride in the Neapolitans: "Yes, yes! Have it as you will; dress them in red, dress them in blue, they will run away all the same." For the support of numbers gives weak men the courage to say and to do that which they feel to be wrong.

Of the part played in literature by the trousers it is difficult to speak, within the limits of the present work, so many and so

important are the instances besides those but
just alluded to.   Yet it is impossible to pass
in silence the one most endeared to the recollection by the exquisite genius and sweet
humanity of Cervantes.   In his inimitable
description of his hero, how lightly he passes
over the other less characteristic portions of
Don Quixote's dress to set before us, with
one touch, the perfect picture of the knight
in his antique dignity and lofty self-posses-
sion, by the mention of his " velvet breeches
of a holiday, and his slippers of the same !"
No one but a master, a literary artist of the
most delicate insight into character, could
have seized so unerringly upon a trait so distinctive and so full of revelation.   How vast
the distance between art so subtle and the
labored catalogue of small details which do
but fatigue the reader without aiding his
perceptions, or enabling him to conceive the
personages in so many of what are called the
novels of real life !   To find anything like
this delicacy we must go to the kindred
genius of Molière, who sets before us at a
stroke the narrow-mindedness and ignorant
prejudice of the dullard who looks upon

women as mere cooks and house-servants, in the immortal lines:

"Une femme en sait toujours assez,
Quand la capacité de son esprit se hausse
A connaître un pourpoint d'avec un haut-de-chausse."

Of later allusions to this most interesting and important subject, the most sufficient is, perhaps, that in Lord Lytton's story of English life, *My Novel.* When Dr. Riccabocca is disrobing himself, with the help of his faithful Giacomo, and confides to him the contemplated marriage with Miss Jemima, the subject is introduced, and the confidence made, in a way that brings into admirable relief the characters of both master and man. "These people," says the doctor, "want me to accept £6000." "Six thousand pounds!" answers Giacomo, pausing in the act of drawing off his master's trousers; "six thousand pounds sterling! A hundred and fifty thousand pounds Milanese!" "Yes; but they want me to do something for it!" says the doctor. "Ah!" cries Giacomo; "these mercenary English! They want you to become a Protestant!" "No," replies Riccabocca, while Giacomo stands with the trousers, fairly drawn off at last, hanging on his arm. "No; they want me never to wear these again." "Never to wear—!" gasps out Giacomo, looking, mouth and eyes wide open, at his master's long, lean legs. This is an admirable scene, with a touch of genuine humor rare in Lytton's voluminous writings, and shows what he might have done if he had not chased so long and so far the will-o'-the-wisp of an intangible philosophy.

The extension of the cylindrical idea, from the trousers to the waistcoat and coat, was a long and slow process. The waistcoat, indeed, must have existed in some form from a very early date, for men must have found, soon after the invention of separate garments in place of the one all-sufficient skin or robe, that a smaller, more closely-fitting piece about the chest and upper portion of the body was imperatively called for. It was, at first, a band wrapped around the body, but this was soon found to be inconvenient, and it was modified, by degrees, from the shape of a loosely-fitting, sleeveless shirt, into what has remained substantially the same form in all places, made now longer, now shorter, cut higher up to the neck or open farther down the front, but always literally a waistcoat, according to the proper English term, a more significant one every way than the French-American word *vest*, since the former clearly identifies, and at the same time defines, the real purpose of this part of the costume, while *vest*, which means only a covering or garment in general, requires a supplementary definition. Nevertheless, between two words, indicating the same article in common use, it will usually be found that the shorter one is almost sure to supplant the longer. The exceptions to this rule are few, and some of them more apparent than real. *Vest* is perceptibly winning in the struggle with its rival.

As the doublet of the earlier time passed into the waistcoat of more modern days, the former name was applied to the coat almost as often as to the close waistcoat. It was at the beginning of the reign of Charles II that the dress of a gentleman is described by Randal Holmes, the Cheshire herald, as quoted by Mr. Planché, in terms which leave no doubt as to the final disappearance of the remains of the picturesque Elizabethan styles: "A short-waisted doublet and petticoat-breeches, the lining being lower than the breeches, is tied above the knees; the breeches are ornamented with ribbons up to the pocket, and half their breadth upon the thigh; the waistband is set about with ribbons, and the shirt hanging out over them." This doublet with the short waist was, in fact, the coat, and by the end of the reign of Charles II it had been lengthened to the middle of the thigh, while its sleeves, reaching only to the elbow, were there joined by the bulging sleeves of the shirt, ruffed, and adorned with ribbons.

Through the reigns of the second Charles, James II, and William III, there was but trifling alteration in costume. The Great King dominated the social as well as the political and the literary world during this long period, the most imposing portion of the costume which he wore being the tremendous periwig created to preserve the tradition of his youthful beauty. The story runs that Louis, when a little boy (he became king at the age of five years), had remarkably beautiful hair, which fell in long waving curls upon his shoulders, and the courtiers, out of compliment to the young majesty, had perukes fashioned to imitate his curls. Mr. Planché considers the story more than doubtful, and it may safely be set down in the category with the famous legend about the change in the gender of the word *carrosse*, made permanently masculine, from feminine that it had been, because the boy-king had commanded *son carrosse*, and the courtiers recognized his authority over the dictionary, as over every other sublunary thing.

CHAPTER XII.

THE discussion of the subject of healthful dress, both for men and women, has been a fruitful as well as a fruitless theme since the earliest ages; and while it is, perhaps, strictly speaking, beyond the domain of the ornamental so fully treated in other parts of this volume, it is of such vital import to man in general that some reflections of the author's experience may be noted here. Without, therefore, venturing on that sanitary ground which is the sole sphere of the physiological expert, it is well to speak of those ordinary conditions of attire inseparable from healthy apparel. These conditions should be apparent to every skilled tailor who understands the physique of his subject, and who is made aware of his bodily infirmities. Still, there are some general observations particularly applicable to America, and illustrating afresh that ignorant spirit of imitation of the useful in England,

in which the pioneers make it the fashion
for fashion's sake, when there is no sensible
reason whatever for importing English styles.
Take, for instance, the ulster. What was its
origin in Great Britain? It was invented,
as other extraordinary garments of those
isles have been, to suit a practical purpose
—one eminently practical, too. Their rail-
way carriages are narrow compartments,
warmed in winter by portable zinc heaters
filled with hot water, and which take a fresh
supply, from time to time, along the route
of travel. As these compartments hold but
six travelers, and there is no space for other
than mere hand-luggage, the ulster was designed to replace the rug, and to permit the
traveler, thus protected against draught and
imperfect heating, to seek repose and sleep
without sprawling out under the cover of
the old devices. For this purpose the ulster
was found to be a most opportune expedient.
Straightway, however, the American intro-
duces it at home. *He* wears it going to the
opera, in the steam and street cars, and
thinks it particularly appropriate at cafés
and walking up and down the avenue, little

knowing that, by this unwieldy and un-
natural heat-producing mass of heavy clothes,
he is undergoing cutaneous exhalations, all
of which are speeding him to the tomb.
Here it is an abuse of the use of a desirable
garment for a specific purpose, but not in
American travel, and most assuredly not in
our every-day life in the cities. This is a
case of the over-wrought. It passes away beyond the bounds of moderation, and reaches
excess; for we can have excess in dress,
in drinking, and in eating. Given a shunt
in any direction, and the American is apt to
be apish, to go to the ultimate extreme.
Who can estimate the useful lessons which
might be derived from Dr. Tanner, who undoubtedly fasted for forty days simply to
show that we, as a people, eat too much?
And, were the subject thoroughly fathomed,
can it be doubted that one of the national
sins against health is baking the body in
an oven fabricated of silk, cotton, chamois,
and wool, thus excluding the air from the
millions of respiratory pores? Is it a won-
der that, since these very ulsters have come
into fashion, old New Yorkers—those who

have stood the wintry blasts of Manhattan
till whitened with years, and who have faced
the biting winds blowing eastward from the
sea, in every-day attire, only to grow ruddier
—have shot out of existence in a few hours,
with their obituaries marked " Pneumonia?"
Let the New Yorker call the mortuary roll
of his friends for a single winter and spring
—those who have been cut down without a
warning—and the brief struggle with the
grim spectre may be assigned to the load of
wraps which he wears and discards at brief
intervals, when the moment of discomfort is
too much for his ease of body. Better, in-
finitely, would it be for a man to wear a
uniform weight of fabrics during all temperatures of the year, rather than swaddle
himself in the manner described. This may
sound as if it were directly against the
tailor's self-interest; if so, so be it, for this,
like Montaigne's book, " is a book of good
faith." But the ills of pneumonia are all
of recent origin—whether they come from
external heat produced from superabundance
of garb, or internally from an excessive use
of spirits. This is the simple truth that can

be seen recorded in the registers of the
public hospitals or the diaries of private
physicians. How different was the story of
necrology of our fathers, who led lives of
simplicity, activity, and physical as well as
mental toil, and were only glad if they could
wear clothes free from rent and soil. There
is the historical anecdote, spread on the public records, of Silas Wright, once governor
of New York State, U. S. senator, and
statesman, whose fame rang through the
world. In his dress and occupation he
looked, in every particular, like a common
laboring farmer. He had the utmost abhorrence for anything like fiction in equipage,
politics, manners, or style of dress; and,
when he returned from his senatorial duties,
he followed the example of Chief Justice
Marshall, and took his wheelbarrow and went
to the village mill to purchase flour and meal.
It so happened that, while governor of the
State, he found himself called to Lockport,
in Western New York, to inspect the im-
provement on the colossal hydraulic works of
the Erie Canal. While climbing up the steep
hill leading from the lower to the upper city,

he came in contact with jagged edges of the craggy rock, and a large rent was the result on his seat of dignity of the bifurcated garment. His Excellency, however democratic, could not proceed without visiting a tailor, who then and there, without process of disrobing, applied a huge patch to the unsightly area. Years later, this incident became political property of a grotesque kind, when it was discovered that he had filed a voucher with the financial officer of the State, upon which he had drawn sixpence from the public treasury to reimburse himself for necessary expenses incurred during an official journey. Statesmen and publicists often have queer notions about dress, and these are generally founded on very erroneous opinions of sanitary laws. The writer recalls a scene which he witnessed in Bordeaux, in France, when the Assembly was called together, at the close of the Franco-German War, to decide whether the nation would submit to the terms of Bismarck. A party of American journalists were taking breakfast together at a private table in the Hotel de France, when a little, beardless and timid man approached a well-known Boston journalist, who rose to receive him in a quiet way.

"Here," said the bashful new-comer, apparently a little frightened on approaching such a fashionably dressed circle, "are two of the best seats for the sitting of the Assembly to-day. It will be a great event in French history. We will decide for continued war against the invaders, or for peace."

A New York journalist of the party was on the alert in an instant, for seats in that tumultuous legislature could not be obtained by dukes, marshals, or even princes, for that historic day. He closely scrutinized the little man, who was clad in baggy trousers, well-worn and ill-fitting sack-coat, and frayed tie, and concluded that he was some favored *commissionaire* of the Assembly without his insignia of service. The enterprising scribe jumped up in eager haste, and, producing a handful of napoleons, said:

"Here we are! Get me two seats, or even one, and this money is yours."

A sudden color mounted to the cheek of the Frenchman, and the Boston journalist bounded back as if he had been struck by a

WINTER.

projectile from a Krupp gun, and the moment
was one of supreme awkwardness. In a short

time, however, the lucky recipient of the tickets stammered forth to his comrades :

" Permit me to make known Mr. Louis Blanc, the distinguished historian of France, and member of the National Assembly."

The effect may be imagined ; but, after mutual explanations, no one enjoyed the *contretemps* more thoroughly than the most renowned orator who then swayed that mercurial body in which sat Thiers, Jules Favre, Gambetta, Rochefort, Grévy, and Jules Simon, not to speak of the commanding form of Garibaldi costumed in his red shirt. But, sad to relate, his very neglect of the simple sanitary rules of dress subsequently cut short the distinguished career of Louis Blanc and carried him over to the majority—the great departed of his race, among whom he stands unequaled in handling the fascinating diction of the French tongue, and one of the finished classical writers and philosophers of his time.

The central idea of healthful dress lies in knowing how to dress to varying temperatures, in a manner to permit equable exhalations from the body, so that the circulation may be ever normal, and particularly so as to protect the exercise of the vital functions. This is not a difficult problem to solve if one obey the Greek injunction " Know thyself." Every man, in studying his own physical susceptibilities, should, in a measure at least, be able to determine the requirements of a protective and agreeable covering. Thus no fixed laws can be laid down; yet in general it may be maintained that there is no excuse for careless exposure, if close attention be given to this subject, and particularly among those of adequate means. The author's experience teaches him that no wardrobe, having a pretence to completeness, is perfect without its owner has at least five different overcoats to meet the fluctuations of the thermometer. First, there should be a very light overcoat for midsummer, for those who make sudden changes from in-doors into the night air, as from the heated theatre to the cool draughts without, or when, as often occurs, there is a sudden change of thirty degrees, from a collar-melting torridity to refrigerating blasts. This may be but little heavier than the ordinary duster, but it serves to shed the north-laden breezes which carry on their wings many a grim

spectre, and myriads of racking coughs which
chase the unfortunate victim oftentimes into a
lingering affection of the lungs, having, more
often than is ever dreamed, the dread termination.   Then there should be the usual light
spring overcoat, when winter has taken its
final leave; and in the autumn one of heavier
make, so graded as to weight that the transition may be gradual to a garment of medium
make which can be worn in late November
and early December, and at times during the
sunny and thawing days of winter. And last,
of course, comes the regular winter overcoat,
which can give freedom to the legs and be
not so heavy as to embarrass locomotion, or
liable, in this climate, to any of the objections
urged against the absurd use of ulsters.   Of
course a precautionary wardrobe like this,
even when wealth permits, cannot always be
had, particularly among naval and army officers on duty, and among those strict ecclesias-
tics who will not on any occasion depart from
the conventional cloth.   *A propos* of this, it
is narrated of President Cleveland's grand-
father—who, besides being a noted preacher,
always in his pulpit uniform, no matter what

the season, was also a hot federalist of the school of Jay and Hamilton—that, while riding horseback in the good old days of 1793, he met a young man coming from the opposite direction along the highway. The divine wished to water his horse in the stream, which they reached at the same moment, but the youth drew his rein so suddenly that the water was roiled and made unfit to drink.

"Good morning, Mr. Minister!" said the bold countryman.

"Good morning, Mr. Democrat!" replied the reverend gentleman.

"And, pray, why did you take me for a democrat?" said the young man.

"Pray, why did you take me for a minister?" rejoined the parson.

"Oh!" said the fellow, "that is plain enough by your *dress*."

"And that you are a democrat is plain enough by your *address*," was the retort of the reverend Cleveland.

On the hygiene of dress a great deal has been written, and many impractical reforms have been suggested to both sexes. Recently there has appeared Dr. G. Jaeger, in a volume called *Health Culture and the Sanitary Woolen System,* in which the learned M.D. would convert us into veritable sheep. The vaulting enthusiast proclaims that we must, or die, unto ourselves a woolen night-shirt take, then woolen socks, and woolen drawers, and woolen wrappers, and woolen coats and caps, and trousers all, and lie down to sleep in woolen beds. Such a being, observing his own laws, will have the wind duly tempered to him, like the shorn lamb, and in the fullness of time he will perform most astonishing vocal exploits ; and the doctor gravely hints that tenors, baritones, contraltos, and sopranos, will spring up in a jiffy, and the world will be submerged by a deluge of song—marvelous youth and longevity, never vouchsafed before his discovery! His earnest attention to, and encomiastic essays on, the virtues of the mutton family, constitute an intellectual effort quite as extraordinary as that of the man who has invented an eating apparatus to relieve the digestive organs of their periodical labor, or the scheme of the man who proposes to reinforce the empty gray cells of the brain with Byronic or Shakespearean phosphorus by an off-hand bit of surgery. And, Doctor:

"'Tis the world's debt to deeds of high degree;
And, if you pay yourself, the world is free."

From what has been advanced, it will be perceived that the hygiene of dress is founded on strict common sense and easily ascertained conditions of the individual. Dark and light clothes govern the methods of the seasons so generally found on this side of the water, and there is little to say within the scope of a volume like this that is not understood by all intelligent men. The one vital principle is—do not overdress; do not weigh yourself down with heavy and useless garments; and be assured that the straight road to longevity lies along the pathway where you find elegant styles and material made only by the best of manufacturers.

CHAPTER XIII.

THE IDEAL SUIT OF CLOTHES.

It is treading on dangerous ground to proclaim fixed standards, or promulgate inflexible laws of fashion. What pleases one gentleman will not another, and, while some are extremists in all that adorns the person, there is a distinct class who prefer the very subdued attire, either as a protest against all manner of ostentation, or because it is the habit of their set. Yet, however this, the guiding principle of the ideal suit lies in one overshadowing word—*outline*. From whatever point of view we observe the figure of man, as clad in the clothes of the period, the bounding curves and profiles must encase a symmetrical being with the laws of proportion strictly followed. Beyond this it is unnecessary to go into the technical art of the cutter and fitter. Let us now inquire how many styles prevailing in 1885 are in to stay—that have taken a firm root among all the peoples of Europe and America. These

comprise four garments—the sack coat, the
frock coat, the four-button cutaway, and the
dress coat. Waistcoats and trousers will constantly change, but the coats are fixed, and
will so remain, with trivial changes, until there
is a total revolution in our apparel. All of
these garments should, therefore, belong to
the wardrobe of every gentleman, even if
he does not go beyond the middle-class social
circles in his contact with fashionable life,
so called. Of these, perhaps, the sack or
lounging coat is the most indispensable, as
it is the easiest, the most desirable in active
bodily movements, and serviceable in nearly
all kinds of business, except where extreme
dignity is required. Of course, men regard
the working suit as one that can be well executed, or badly, according to the service
required, and extremes are shown in the
following:

"Why don't you wash and dress yourself
when you come into a court of justice?" asked
a pompous begowned and bewigged London
judge of a chimney-sweep, who was being
examined as a witness.

"Dress myself, my Lord!" said the sweep.

"I am dressed as much as your Lordship. I'm in my *working* clothes, and you are in yours."

The frock coat, so commonly known in the United States as the Prince Albert, is a misnomer when spoken of as the supposed creation of the Queen's Consort. It existed long before he did, and will continue to prevail long after we are all gathered to our fathers. It is exactly suited to its purpose—that of afternoon or early evening wear; and not till the era so earnestly predicted by Oscar Wilde and his disciples will it give way to another. But the neatest, and really the nattiest, garment that has come into vogue in recent years, is the four-button cutaway. Has a man a good figure, it exhibits in a perfect manner, and with flowing and graceful lines, the fullness of the chest, the firm lines of the shoulders, the inward curves of the back, as well as the tapering body to the hips. Regarded in profile, in front or behind, it is always shapely, sitting easily on the figure with scarcely an angle to be found. Contrast this even with the double-breasted frock, and the latter suffers because of its rectangular aspect and superabundance of cloth. And here let it be remarked that men should not go about carrying superfluous fabrics. The aim of men's wear should be protection, simplicity, style in the cut, and so designed as to make the best of all of the advantages and defects of the figure. As to the dress-suit, there have been recent attempts to improve it, particularly by the fashion journals of England; and, while progress would doubtless be of great advantage to tailors, it cannot be honestly said that any advance has been made beyond publishing plates and descriptions of the newly designed garment. In brief, the upper portion of the coat, down to the flaps, closely resembles the present evening dress coat, with the curved line extending from the lower termination of the lapels to the extreme trails reaching above the knees behind. The designers insist that this can be made up in blue, black or wine color, to supersede the existing style, or, in default of that, it should be worn for promenade wear. This is mentioned, not because it is likely to come into immediate use, but to exhibit the restlessness which gentlemen all

over the world feel in their eager desire to
bury forever that costume of all dress occasions which makes gentlemen and servants
outwardly the same.   Hundreds of ludicrous
situations have occurred in the experience of
every man of the world, and some of them
decidedly dramatic and tragic, where our
conventional "claw-hammer" has produced
life-long enmities.

The author has often been asked how
much should a gentleman spend on his wardrobe annually?   Allowing that he has the
general tastes of a man about town—one of
leisure, interested in lawn sports and athletic
games, a gentleman rider, following yachting
and hunting, and fishing, with all of the
winter amusements included, and that he is
possessed of a wardrobe covering all the
differing fields of pleasure—it will require the
sum of $500 a year to replenish the articles
that go into disuse, and keep the various
suits in repair.   This is an economical estimate for a man of fashion, and one who is not
wasteful or extravagant.   But there are men
of large means in this city, who own their
stud, their yacht and kennel, who order as

many as fifty suits of clothes at a time; and there is one gentleman in New York, not yet thirty-five years of age, and of a slenderer bank account than an ordinary cutter, who boasts of having two hundred and fifty suits

STYLES THAT WILL STAY.

of clothes, all made by the same London tailor. As the aim of this volume throughout has been to be honest with the reader, regardless of consequences (for, after all, that is the easiest way), it may be said that to

expend over $1000 annually in enlarging
and replenishing the wardrobe is nothing
more nor less than sheer folly. There are
many obvious exceptions to this, as with
actors or amateur theatrical performers, or
those who belong to lodges, regiments or
societies. Notwithstanding the truth of this
estimate, there are hundreds of New Yorkers
who far exceed this outlay, and perhaps,
in the majority of cases, no word should be
written to discourage them. We refer to
those who never wear a suit once soiled or
out of shape, but who send it to their butlers,
valets, and other serving men. This is widely
prevalent in the better circles, and accounts
for the fact that "swell" cooks, doormen,
coachmen and waiters, are so often as well
dressed as their masters. There is a waiters'
and cooks' club in Lexington avenue, as there
is a resort where they convene in Sixth avenue, and the visitor there for the first time is
startled to find such a well-dressed body of
men. Indeed, there cannot be found, at any
club in the city, a body so uniformly well
attired as when these servitors don their
fine feathers.

It is aside from the object of a treatise like this, which does not pretend to disclose the technique of clothes-making, to go to any extent into the business operations of the merchant-tailor. But there are several features in relation to the class of manufacture which it is proposed to notice briefly. First, every superior tailor should be his own cutter. He should not permit his business to grow to such an extent that, in this respect, he should not be able to undertake the fashioning of each separate garment before it is handed out for manufacture. The author has never deviated from this rule, here or elsewhere, nor should any one in the vanguard of the guild. Again, he not only should make the patterns—that is, design and cut them himself, but, moreover, he should cut the cloth. There is a knack in this that does not come to every one, and few journeymen can be trusted to do it to perfection. This involves the knowledge of fabrics, of their fibres and stretching qualities, and whether to cut inside or outside the line of demarcation. If the reader will consider how difficult all of this is when

varying physiques perplex the judgment, he
will understand how necessary it is to have
accurate patterns of each man's frame, exactly
as the shoe-maker makes and keeps a last for
a standing customer. It thus happens that
tailors are often consulted by sculptors as to
the dimensions of a distinguished man who
has passed away, and who is to be put in
bronze in some public place. Again, no first-
class manufacturer will employ women to
make the garments, and by this we do not
intend to disparage feminine agility or ex-
pertness. The gentler sex are better adapted
to dress-making, and this being their peculiar
sphere, they should not take it as a reflection
when we say that men's clothes can be better
made by men.

Fabrics, of themselves, would make an interesting book. But we do not intend to
lengthen our observations by going into the
manufacture of woolens, any more than we
would consider it necessary to explain the
technique of picture-painting in order to present the startling beauties of the composition
or the intelligent industry of the artist. All
that is pertinent to say is, that those leaders

of style among the tailors of New York who
make only first-class clothes are forced to
buy only English goods, because, unpatriotic
as it may be to say so, American manufacturers cannot yet produce cloths of equal
beauty, fibre, and texture, with all other
durable qualities, when competing with the
English. And with this inferiority of the
domestic article in view, the expense of English goods, with the *ad valorem* duty of forty
per cent. added, besides the thirty-five cents
per pound specific duty, renders the English
fabric quite as expensive as that sold here.
People often ask, when keeping this subject
in mind, why it is that Fifth avenue tailors
demand and get the large prices they do.
Let us answer, because they buy only the
best of material in England, while inferior
craftsmen import the cheaper stuffs. You
can buy woolens in England for 2s. 6d. to
24s. a yard, but the latter is the figure paid
by the best tailors on the avenue. And it is a
fact that a $100 suit of clothes sold at retail
in New York actually costs the tailor $75
outlay. The three garments cost, for the
stitches alone, $21 ; for the cloth, $28 ; for the

cutting and trimming, upward of $25. Often the alterations will cost from $3 to $5.

One may well ask, then, where does the tailor's profit come from? In part, from the cutting; for in England there is a saying, that the cutter who cannot save his wages, in the handling of the shears with a view to economy, had better quit the business. These shoppy details and reflections have been made to show that the highway to the ideal suit of clothes is not a royal road; but, with the best of cloth, artistic designing, accurate cutting, close fitting, and a thorough knowledge of the physique of the dresser, no man who is a tailor can fail to attain highly creditable results.

CHAPTER XIV.

There have always been, and there always will be, beaux; and it ought to be noted that the received idea as to the emptiness and use-lessness of the character is like a great many other received ideas that will not bear ex-amination. If the young Roman dandies in Pompey's army at Pharsalia turned their backs for fear their beauty should be spoiled, and we have no evidence but that of their enemies for the statement, the gay young nobles of France flung themselves on the cold steel of the English infantry, and the Iron Duke acknowledged that, with all their shortcomings, "the London puppies fought well." It may be stated, as an axiom, that no man can be a genuine beau without possessing some intellectual or moral force to carry him to the front. If it is objected that there have been famous leaders of fashion de-ficient in force of will and mind, the answer suggests itself; the record is a defective one,

and the world does not really know its beaux.
Take, for instance, the type that comes first
to the recollection, Beau Brummel.   In the
infinite number of anecdotes related of him,
very few are in any way creditable to his
heart, but there is the stamp on nearly every
one of a strong will and a keen and ready
wit.   He was asked if he had been intimate
with William IV, while yet Duke of Clarence,
and in the navy.   "I cannot say I was," he
answered.   "The man did very well to wear a
cocked hat, and walk about the quarter-deck
crying 'Luff!'   But he was so rough and un-
civilized that I was obliged to cut him."   Like
this, in insolence and readiness, was his reply,
when in exile at Caen, to the question whether
he had attended the ball given by the city in
honor of Louis Philippe's visit.   Brummel
was an ultra conservative in politics, and detested the monarchy of July.   "The King's
ball?" he asked.   "What king?"   "What
king?   The French king, to be sure; Louis
Philippe."   "Oh!" said Brummel, "you mean
the Duke of Orleans.   No; I did not go, but
I sent my servant."   We may find various
unamiable qualities in the man who made

these remarks, but they imply real force. Not every leader of fashion was equal to Brummel, but some were superior to him in mind and character, and almost all had real gifts to make them not unworthy of their place. Where, in modern times, are we to find a greater dandy than the famous minister of Augustus III of Saxony and Poland, Count Brühl, with his four hundred dresses, his luxurious table, his milk poultices to preserve the delicacy of his complexion? But his taste was equal to his love of dress, and the Dresden Gallery was almost the work of his master and himself.

Talleyrand was not less a dandy than a diplomatist. When Lord Sefton went to see him he found the Prince in the hands of two *valets de chambre*, while a third, who was training for his duties in this line, looked on at what was done. The Prince was in a loose flannel gown; his long locks, which were rather scanty, were twisted and *crépus* with a curling-iron, saturated with powder and pomatum, and then arranged with great care into snowy ringlets. When the news of Napoleon's landing at Cannes reached Vienna,

where the Congress was in session, the des-
patch was brought to Talleyrand by his
niece, who was to attend a ball that night.
The Prince was, at the moment, having himself perfumed with essences by his valet, and
bade his niece open the dispatch. She read
it out: "Napoleon has escaped from Elba,"
and let the paper drop, with the exclama-
tion: "Good heavens! And my ball!" "Say
nothing, my child," calmly replied Talleyrand,
holding out his hands to the valet; "you shall
have your ball." Not the just man in Horace's
ode was more unmoved in the crash of the
universe than this crafty schemer and exquisite. His Austrian counterpart, Metternich,
was equally high-bred and refined, and careful of the proprieties and elegances of costume.
It is enough to name two or three of these
celebrated leaders, to refute the crude and
hasty generalizations which associate attention to dress with incapacity for matters
conventionally called serious.

Of beaux among modern princes the house
of Orleans has had at least two very remarkable ones, the Regent, and his great-grandson
Egalité. The profligate career of the Regent

should not blind us to the fact that he was a master in the art of dress, and knew how to bring to bear upon style in costume his accomplishments as a painter and engraver. Egalité deserves especial remembrance as a startling innovator rather than as a model of elegant dressing, and yet his taste stamped him, no less than his courage, in leading the inevitable movement toward the more simplified costume. He was the first noble to set the fashion of wearing pantaloons instead of breeches, and boots instead of low shoes with buckles, and to discard hair-powder. It is true that when he was borne to his execution he powdered his hair in the old high-bred style, and went to meet death with a serene courage that would have redeemed even a worse career than his.

The reign of Anne brought in a style of costume in England that made fine dressing more difficult than it had ever been, so ungraceful were the outlines and the shapes. It was not easy for any one to look his best in a square-cut coat and long-flapped waistcoat, the skirts of the coat stiffened out with wire or buckram, with a sword looking out between the skirts, square-toed shoes, and long curled perukes crowned by small three-cornered hats. There was little of the æsthetic in the line of the Georges, and the services rendered by them to English taste in attire have been of very little account. George the Fourth is, of course, the only one of the line who seems to claim especial recognition as a man of fashion and genuine appreciation of good dressing, but one is inclined to think, on examination of the matter, that his reputation has been in a great measure made for him, and that his personal contributions to the progress of this art have by no means equaled those of many a less famous man. Brummel made much of the Prince's renown as an arbiter of fashion. "The Prince," said a famous tailor, "wears superfine, and Mr. Brummel the Bath coating; it is immaterial which you choose, Sir John; suppose we say the Bath coating—I think Mr. Brummel has a trifle the preference." This was stating the case mildly, as became a loyal Briton, for society gave the Beau a decided preference. The Prince has been so often the subject of biographers and essayists that it is probable we see very little of the real man. He has been praised and abused without let or stint, and most persons think of him as the " fat friend," pinched in his tight clothes, and considerably disguised with drink. Fortune was unkind to him in one respect, at least. If he had not been a Prince, and a King, he would have left a less contemptible name ; but he has secured an immortality of a kind, since no one can cast a glance over the history of European cos- tume without taking in George IV. He had the merit, also, of wishing to have done something in active life, and a vanity that would have the facts give way to its per- sistent whim, as in his famous delusion, the result of assiduous lying on the subject, that he had been present at Waterloo. His ap- peal to Wellington is well known : " You remember, Arthur, how I led that charge ?" " I remember having heard your Majesty say so," was all that could be got from the Duke. Vanity of this sort is admirable in its way, and, if the King had not been so fat, and could have kept sober, he might have done real service to the cause of scientific dress-

ing.   His career stretches over the gulf between the last days of the French monarchy
and the new order of things after the over-
throw of Napoleon.   In that time the
changes in France were bewildering, in costume as in politics.   At the court of Louis
XVI dressing was the serious business of the
day.   The Comte de Provence, afterward
Louis XVIII, was too fond of his Horace and
his table to be a leader of fashion, but
d'Artois, who became Charles X, was an exquisite, entirely devoted to dress, flirting, and
hunting.   When his breeches were to be put
on—he wore them very tight—this was the
process: Four valets took their places in
due order; two held the breeches open at a
proper height; the other two, always tall
and powerful men, raised the Prince from the
floor and lowered him gradually into the garment, until it fitted like a second skin.   It is
not recorded that the Comte d'Artois used
this style of breeches for sitting in ; but the
gallants of the day dressed as he did.   The
visit of Franklin to this brilliant court produced an extraordinary effect.   Ribbons and
laces, curls and embroidery, disappeared as

if by magic, and nothing was to be seen but straight-cut hair and straight brown coats. Just before the Revolution broke out, the hat began to show itself in the round up-right shape which has sat upon the heads of mankind ever since, like an extinguisher of all grace. The changes under the Revolution were like the shapes in a kaleidoscope. The Athenians, the Romans, the *incroyables*, the *merveilleux*, the hair worn *à la Titus*, the dresses *à la Cybèle*, and a thousand other ex-travagant costumes and parts of costumes culminating in the dress *à la sauvage*, that is, in no dress at all, made an assemblage of French people look like a party of escaped lunatics. The Empire reduced all this to order of a formal and administrative kind, but Napoleon had his mind too much occu-pied with other grave concerns to give to dress the attention it demanded.

The democratic constitution of society at this period, immediately succeeding the wild fervor of the Revolution, was, moreover, un-favorable to a cultivated taste in dress, and in place of elegance there was the plainness affected by Napoleon, and the theatrical display of Murat, King Franconi. The English taste has prevailed more and more in France since the Restoration, with the interruption of the second Empire, with its extravagant parade and ostentation. It is not a little remarkable to find that courts so splendid as those of Austria, Russia, and Germany, have counted for nothing in their influence on costume. With all their resources they have been content to take the law from France and England, which are the two arbiters of modern fashion, the predominating influence to-day being the English. This is personified in the Prince of Wales, who can hardly be said to create, so much as he stands for, the English taste, since this was as clearly the prevailing taste before he came upon the scene as it has been since. In truth, one great purpose served in English civilization by the Prince of Wales is that he presents a type, visible to all, and recognizable, of the tendencies in costumes. To know what is the right thing to wear, men have but to look at the embodiment of the artistic ideas in the person of the heir-apparent; and the dignity of his station and position gives to his example an irresistible force which but few written edicts possess. Leaders of fashion there will be—under him; but it may be accepted as a sound conclusion that there will be no Beau Brummel to dispute pre-eminence with a future Prince of Wales. The movement toward simplicity in dress has gone so far, that we may anticipate the future undisturbed rule in fashion of the heir to the monarchy.

CHAPTER XV.

GOING TO THE TAILOR.

De l'usage de se vêtir.—MONTAIGNE.

WHEN you make up your mind to go to your tailor, be sure and take some friend whose critical faculty has reached the most extreme development. Mind you, he must be an arch-pessimist, who accepts nothing on the say-so. If your companion be one of the other sex, take pains that she has passed the enthusiastic days of youth; that her jaws are square and firmly set, her eyes steel-gray and gifted with an arctic scrutiny, and her mandate never to be disputed. All artist-tailors warm to, and, indeed, hanker after such assistant patrons. Their lives would be miserable without they crossed the door-sill daily. Notice the cheerful smile and urbane manners with which your tailor mentally sums up your companion's capacity for detail. He perceives he is in for a prolonged professional séance, and although well-nigh profitless in the end, he is aware that he will be taught, in several editions of caustic volubility, how to become a real maker and fitter. Your demeanor throughout should be quiet, with an outspoken and definite purpose to have a good suit of clothes of the most fashionable cut and fabric. The goods are inspected in detail, and finally you select a pleasing pattern, with "I think that will do!"

"Why, my dear," exclaims your companion, "you can get a much handsomer check at Blank, Blank & Co.'s, and think of a nice watch thrown in."

"True, Janet," is the response; "but you know I never wear ready-made clothing."

"If you will permit me, madame," interposes the merchant, meekly," there is a vast difference between the durability, and other indispensable qualities, of cloths used in the different grades of our business. A lady of your excellent judgment would certainly not wish to have your husband attired in apparel that would have one color to-day, a blending of shades to-morrow, and none at all on the third. Nor would you care to have his shapely figure deformed by a costume of a kind in every way unsuited to a gentleman."

A look of calm satisfaction lights up the countenance of his patron, but Janet is not to be mollified or cajoled by **any such** specious talk as this—not she.

"Such statements," she maintains, "are all very well, when coming from tailors who are simple money-makers, any way; but I do not see why you cannot get just as good clothes at any house, on Sixth avenue, or on Eighth avenue, for less than one-half the money, as you can here in Fifth avenue."

"Madame," the tailor responds, with deference, "you can, of course, buy garments at the places and prices you name. So you can get your dinner in Sixth avenue for fifteen cents, and one with the same name at Delmonico's for a dollar and a half."

"These goods, then, are so much superior to the others?"

"They are. No first-class tailor will carry in his stock an imitation or fraudulent article, any more than would Tiffany undertake to manufacture for you a set of bogus jewelry, or to set a ton of Parisian diamonds."

You now announce your intention to stand by your first choice, when Janet says:

"But remember, Gus, I am to have a new circular, and where will the money come from?"

And thus, after Janet has ventilated herself thoroughly as to price and pattern, and in quite diplomatic language set the merchant down as a heartless sharp, it is settled that the measure shall be taken and the suit shall be fitted before being made up. The day is appointed, and you sail forth to the tailor's, and stand encumbered with a sleeveless coat, a single trouser, and a quantity of thread, chalk, canvas, and all of the mysteries that go to make form and outline. Your watchful Janet is with you. She is not pleased with the cutter's work at all; the ensemble is too much that of a gambler; the trousers are too suggestive of the dude,—they should be twice as large; when it is perceived that the cloth will not admit of such a radical change. The coat has the waist too low; the collar is not stylish,—it must be enlarged; and the shoulders are too absurd for anything.

"What a pity it is," observes Janet, "that

tailors have no eyes for proportion. It is true there are exceptions sometimes, as in the case of my lamented father, whose tailor in East Broadway made him look spick-and-span!"

The tailor may get a little nervous at this; but what matters that, he has no sensibilities. Janet insisting upon literal obedience to her alterations, you take your departure, awaiting the day of readiness. It soon arrives, and again you invade the shop. You stand up before mirrors, which reflect every angle and curve of your body, and now you are to be the satisfied one. To your horror, you stand in about as cranky a suit of clothes as could be devised by the joint and perverse ingenuity of man and woman. You behold your ghastly smile in the pier-glass, a cold sweat overspreads your body, and, with awakening mind, you draw the true moral of the advantage of having outside advice when you go to your tailor for an outfit of fashionable garments.

Let the law, then, be laid down, for tailors and purchasers alike, that there are no articles figuring in merchandise which should be the subject of sole agreement between maker and patron to a greater extent than the garments constituting men's wear. No outside views should be invited or received.

THE CRITICAL FRIEND.

Your adviser has not got to wear the clothes; they do not concern his comfort or presentability; and, furthermore, the philosopher has told us, truly, "There is something in the *mal-aise* of our best friends which does not displease us." In the experience of every one, who has been many years in the craft, there are hundreds of anecdotes that could be told of the purely malicious suggestions of apparent friends to those purchasing clothing; but this curious phase of human nature, let it be said, belongs oftener to women than to men. The true way, therefore, is to go to that maker who has your confidence, ascertain for what purpose you want your suit of clothes, and leave the designing to him; otherwise, you will share the fate of many others who have called in the layman's aid in this important matter of dressing in fashionable garments.

> " A few are good; some well enough:
> But most, I own, are wretched stuff."

Allusion has been made elsewhere to the selection of a good tailor, and this task is regarded by many gentlemen as very difficult; yet it is not so. It is a very simple matter to understand that those who have won distinction for the finest work are governed in their prosperity by the same laws of supply and demand which relate to the other arts, or to similar kinds of merchandise. You will therefore find those who belong to the topmost round grouped about the fashionable part of the city in close proximity to the hotel centre, and, in New York, tenanting modern mansions which have been refitted for their special uses on Fifth avenue; and the greater the prosperity, and the more refined the taste, of the tailor, the more attractive will be found his shop. *Noblesse oblige;* and the higher the walk in life, and the higher attainments in that walk, the greater the responsibilities. Let us visit one of these shops, or, if the American citizen prefers it, one of the " swell stores." Those of the superlative, of the best form, are nearly all on Fifth avenue, and, in some cases, are owned by their tenants, and the space occupied for the goods and cutters would rent at from $5000 to $7000 a year. The entrance in almost all cases is up a flight of steps to what was formerly the parlors. This front room, facing on the avenue, is devoted to a share of the best imported

fabrics, while further back may be found
the dressing-room, the cutter's table, and all
the paraphernalia of the guild. You may
enter at almost any hour of the day, and
you will rarely meet more than several customers, because one of this class of pro-
prietors considers himself as doing a thriving
business if he takes a half dozen orders a
day. Such a patronage he is better pleased
with than a perfect avalanche of customers;
for he can give his personal attention to
every garment that leaves the shop, and see
that each one is thoroughly satisfied. Wan-
dering, for instance, through the author's
spacious parlors, we found the walls hung
with costly pictures from the studios of
celebrated foreign and American artists.
There we find a superb Corot, showing all
the delicate tree and shrub forms, and mysterious and poetical sky effects, which made
the great French painter one of the masters
of the salon; and beyond is a superb Diaz,
one of those minutely drawn and clearly
expressed land-and-water-scape compositions,
meadowlike in prevailing color, with an atmosphere that carries the feeling that, for its

absolute noiselessness, you can hear the hum of distant bees and clear notes of remote chimes ringing out on the sun-lit air. Then there is the masterpiece of the American painter, Edgar M. Ward,—a large out-doors representing a grouping at Pontaven in Brittany, in which those strong peasant types stand out with miraculous boldness and spirit. There is a winter, too, by Macy, with the leafless branches and snow-covered trunks, the true spirit of Christmas-tide, when

> " The Yule-log burns,
> Loud sounds the horn
> That echoes in
> Christ's natal morn."

J. G. Brown, with his tatterdemalion characters, an example of which is *Used Up*, and others of equal celebrity, adorn the apartments. We behold English park scenery, lone situations, cavaliers, and a great variety in figure and landscape art.

How different all of this, where you can linger among gems like these, and sit patiently down to have yourself taken in hand by a true artist who can appreciate your

needs, from a visit to one of the crowded ma-
chine clothes establishments, to receive scant
attention, to be told that the first garment
snatched up is a perfect fit, and then to quit
the store with your purchase without remedy
against the sudden collapse of your suit, the
falling off of the buttons, the fading of the
colors, the ripping of the seams—and that
feeling of profound disgust that you have
exchanged your good money for worthless
trash.

CHAPTER XVI.

A SUBJECT so wide and vast as the present must be barely more than touched upon in some of its aspects, and to do even this requires a severe limitation of the field. Antiquity must be left out, the middle ages must be passed over, and modern times must be treated as beginning with the Declaration of Independence. How far this manner of looking at the subject may be the right one, must be left to the reader's judgment to decide—but it can be justified. The remains of antiquity, relating to a society and a civilization so unlike our own, have special claims upon our attention for their intrinsic worth and beauty; but, so far as they are held up as types for artists to imitate, they have had a depressing effect upon modern art, and have made the conventional take the place, in the minds of students, that should have been occupied by the truthful and the natural. This is particularly true of modern sculp-

tors, most of whom work with the fear of
Greece before their eyes, as indeed they
should, so far as the fear of Greece means
the admiration of what is best, and the dread
of doing a work unworthy to be studied.
But when this fear means only a servile imitation of costumes and of details for modern
figures, which are appropriate only in the
statues of antiquity, it is a fear fatal to any
real excellence. We have but to glance at
the statues in what is called antique costume,
set up all over the land, to feel that, whatever the shortcomings and the imperfections
of the Greek and Roman world, whatever
the sins and the expiation that came upon
the heathen, much at least was spared to
them; they could not foresee the deplorable
things that were to be called "Statues after
the Antique." The painters have been more
fortunate than the sculptors. The Greek
paintings have perished; and even though
there are all the masterpieces of the great
schools to keep the artists of to-day under
their shadow, the element of color asserts
itself in behalf of every one who paints, and
the works, warm with the light of to-day, at·

tract and gain the ready sympathies of the spectator, who does not feel himself called upon for an effort of the imagination in order to grasp what is set before him. This seems to be an undeniable truth, that holds good even in what should bring out an independent play of mind in the artist, because its very limitations make his task more easy; that is, in portrait sculpture. Why is it that, even when the statue of a modern man is dressed in modern costume, such as the original wore, the figure is made to testify that, if it were alive, it could not walk?—and dressed in modern costume he should be, in his statue, if that was the costume he wore in life. The opinion of an artist-tailor is the right one in this matter. Men do not, nowadays, believe in demi-gods, or sons of Venus and Anchises, but in men like themselves, living and working in the white light of the real day; and when it is proposed to set up the memorial figure of a man, how heroic soever, the first condition to be met is that the figure shall be the counterfeit presentment of the real man. Washington, as he sits on his long box, in the ground behind

the capitol, glowering at Persico's Columbus
playing bowls, is an astonishment and a con-
fusion to the beholder. What tailor, proficient
in his art, would have accepted such a figure
for his private collection of art-works? Yet
Greenough holds himself high as a sculptor
and was at one time the best we could
show in his line, and would have felt himself
insulted, if he had been advised to take counsel with a tailor. The old proverb about
the cobbler confining himself to his last is
sure to be quoted on such occasions, and
nearly always, as if it could have but one
meaning.

It has, on the contrary, two meanings.
The sculptor, as his unlucky figures declare,
undertakes continually to cobble where he
has no skill, and to know better than the
real artist. When he has succeeded in putting
down the tailor who criticises the head of
the statue, he turns complacently round and
puts a coat on the figure of a cut that would
make a living man who wore it the laughing-
stock of the street. It is true that sculptors
can be made to learn in these matters, for
some things can be done as well as others;

but then some men will not do them. Look,
for instance, at .the monuments set up in

THE TRUE ARTIST-TAILOR.

Union Square, and compare, if you have the
heart to do it, any other with Bartholdi's

Lafayette, the only one among them that could, if suddenly endowed with life, get down and walk off unassisted.

The art of the costumer is simplifying the labor of painters and sculptors, by making the fashionable dress less of a disguise than it has been. The padded shoulders have ceased to be characteristic of American dress, the flapping skirts have gone to the limbo of forgotten things, the trousers no longer resemble the windsail of an ocean steamer. The American, properly attired, looks now, from whichever side seen, like a being constructed on the right anatomical principles, which must be known by every artist that attempts to design the human form or to clothe it; and it should be easy to make each of these aid, instead of embarrassing, the other.

It will be said that the tailor has to make the best of an ill-shaped man, and give him a good appearance, while the sculptor or the painter must present a historical character with all his warts, as Cromwell expressed it. There is but a little truth in this. The sculptor may give all the ugly points of his subject, but, as a matter of fact, he generally does nothing of the kind. Take a well-known historical occasion in the life of Lincoln. Most New Yorkers will recall his famous debate with Stephen A. Douglas at Cooper Institute, before he had been thought of as a candidate for the Presidency. When the evening came, Lincoln appeared on the platform in an old, creased broadcloth suit, dusty with travel, for he had but just reached the city; long and awkward looking, he presented a very unfavorable contrast to the Little Giant, as people then delighted to call Douglas, and the Young Men's Christian Association began to think the evening was to be a failure; but, when his moment came, Lincoln amazed everybody by the force and vigor of his speech, and the effort of that night secured his nomination. If a sculptor were charged to reproduce this scene, would he make the shabby clothes in marble? Clearly not, for the shabbiness was not part of the force that carried Lincoln through that night. The sculptor would represent the man as nearly as he could, and bring out in the statue whatever good point he found in his model,—that is to say, he would idealize, so as to make his subject the more real; and this is what the tailor-artist does with the forms that come into his hands. In each case the man is made to appear at his best, but the best, as the artist sees it, really exists in the model. It is the old story, of the eye seeing what it brings with it the power to see. "Mr. Turner," said a lady to the great painter, "I don't see the effects in nature that you put into your pictures." "Don't you wish you could?" replied Turner.

The conclusion forced upon us by the study of the treatment of dress in art is that the artist should represent only what is true to the time and the subject. He should keep to the facts of costume as much as to the facts of anatomy and of physiognomy, and no more; and then, with conscientious study of his task, and the due admixture of brains with his materials, he must produce work that will deserve and achieve renown. It is easy to say, as men often do say, that the age is unpoetical, and that the costume of to-day does not lend itself to heroic treatment. This is the excuse of mere mediocrity, unequal to a struggle with the actual, because it has no insight into the ideal. The heroic and the poetical are permanent elements in every society, and a great character will dignify every and any costume, if only this be the work of an artist.

CHAPTER XVII.

THE REIGN OF THE BRASS BUTTON.

PARADOXICAL as it may seem, America presents at once the best and the worst field for him of the brass button. Boast as we may of our love of peace, our attachment to liberty and all its homely insignia, our fidelity to the industrial arts, and consequent abhorrence of life in the barracks, yet the American is fond of military pageantry, and men, women, and children, will swarm the streets to view a passing regiment, while an 'army corps of thirty thousand veteran troops, marching to stirring national music, in a European capital, will hardly attract the attention of passing pedestrians along the thoroughfare. Yet, true it is, our martial spectacles are sorry parades compared with those of the Old World, and every unbiased traveler must admit this unpalatable truth. While much of our deficiency is due to meagre numbers, the apparent shabbiness of armed commands comes solely from the plebeian cut and fabric of the citizen or regular soldiery. Our spirit of imitation of European uniforms and accoutrements, vaguely carried out, leaves us no distinct and national costume for the army and navy; but, following the stupid innovations and absurd inventions of the bureaucracy at Washington, we have scarcely, in the present age, been able to produce a martial figure in becoming toggery that has not looked awkward and unsightly to the European eye. On the principle that what is worth doing at all is worth doing well, the American soldier, when in juxtaposition with his European confrère, is a signal failure as to his uniform. Why this is true is easily explained. Every change of administration brings a new Secretary of War, and generally a civilian. The same is true of the navy. Then the contractors hive at the capital. Boards of officers of the sere-and-yellow-leaf grades are detailed to report progressive wear for officers and men, and the changes made must needs be a fresh invasion of their pay-accounts. The official tinkering done, the dressier officers of both branches of the service accept the unhappy situation. With many subdued growls we try to tide over the financial inroads by ingenious patch-work of weather-beaten uniforms. There is thus no symmetry as to any single costume, either in cut, color, or decoration, nor does the command present a homogeneous aspect. Singular is all this, when it is conceded that Americans are the most practical and inventive people of the earth, and notably in nearly all that pertains to naval and military creation, to our splendid field hospital service, adopted by nearly all the armies of the world; our life-destroying *mitrailleuses*, our Remingtons, Hotchkiss and other rifles, and breech-loading cannon, our torpedoes, and floating rams, and river gunboats. One would think that, the smaller the military and naval establishments of an opulent power, the greater the care in this matter of presenting an admirably dressed army of soldiers and sailors. But it has not been, and seemingly will not be, until the authorities come down to a correct appreciation of the necessities of good taste and artistic design. Even as it stands, the militia regiments are far better uniformed than the regulars, as the observer can notice at any public occasion, when they appear together in New York. Perhaps it may be argued that this disinclination to follow a careful standard in military dress is to be encouraged, because so many distinguished American generals have set the example. This cannot be regarded as otherwise than pernicious reasoning. It may be an extremely poetic situation to hand down to history, the scene at Appomattox, when Grant, swordless, with a rusty cavalry hat, and a fatigue blouse, advanced to receive the surrender of Lee, who was carefully attired in an elegant uniform; but even the victorious commander himself has confessed that his appearance in crude garb was accidental, wanting in circumspection, and very unsoldierlike. The dignity of the occasion, certainly in its results one of the momentous of modern times, is stripped of its military significance by an absence of ceremonial which is taught to every graduate of West Point and the Naval Academy as one of the very chief essentials of the profession of arms.

"If nature has not given you self-con-

fidence and a decisive bearing," says the
text-book of these institutions, "you must
affect them; you must pretend to a commanding exterior, and give the semblance
of superiority by all outward arts." Recall
some of the recent noteworthy episodes in
European wars, and it will be seen that, by
the etiquette on such occasions as that of
which Grant was the central figure, the
scene was made memorable by a splendor of
military trappings suitable to a great and
decisive event. There was Napoleon III at
Sedan, handing his sword to the King of
Prussia, to mark the extinction of his empire,
yet still the onward march to democracy;
while its reception by the Hohenzollern potentate was to note the beginning of an era
when a liberal monarchy was to assume the
shackles of a far-reaching military State,
with its Emperor crowned in the palace of
Louis XIV at Versailles.

The question then is, what remedy must
be devised to better uniform our officers and
men? This certainly lies with the depart-
ments at Washington; with an intelligent
and liberal action of Congress; but, more than

all, with a united sentiment in the army and navy themselves. In the higher grades the example should be set to junior officers, and no slovenliness in make-up or quality

Time was when the music of the drum,.... and now will he lie ten nights awake, carving the fashion of a new doublet.—

Much Ado About Nothing.

should be permitted. It is not to be wondered at in a squadron, where the admiral goes about utterly regardless of neat and regulation dress, that he cannot enforce a style which can command the respect of foreign officers. This general laxity and neglect has grown up to a large extent since the civil war, for in the olden days our senior officers were as superbly attired as any in the world. Retrogression should, therefore, cease, and practical steps be taken to make our naval officers appear as they did in the days of Goldsborough, Dupont, and Buchanan. Moreover, many years have not passed since army and navy officers were proud to appear among civilians dressed in their appropriate uniforms, precisely as they do in Europe; but now all of this is changed, and it is rare to see either branch of the service in its proper insignia among those in citizen life. When it is so, an American admiral looks like a sergeant of the metropolitan police, and an army colonel like a military instructor at a boarding-school. In the former days, when the wooing was done in blue coats and brass buttons, and all of the other suitable and becoming paraphernalia, the conquest was rapid, and many a portionless midshipman or second lieutenant of the engineers chose his partner for life from among the belle-heiresses of the land—to the discomfiture of those whose accomplishments lay in Wall street lore or among the bales of dry-goods. Now, this has nearly all passed away, as a prominent feature of our social life in America. What ambitious American girl now wants to wed a poor lieutenant in an alleged navy, or go forth to live in shabby barracks on the plains, with nothing to suggest romance in the life of her liege save paltry Indian wars, or the idle gossip of a frontier camp? No! The man of affairs has come to the front. His very style, even in the fashionable wear of the period, far outshines that of the gilt-braided and brass-bespangled defender of Uncle Sam. When it is considered, too, that no officer can enter either branch of the line without undergoing a stringent physical examination, it will be perceived that he has the average civilian at a very considerable disadvantage. Knock-knees, bow-legs, bantam bodies, and deformed neck and shoulders, are not admitted into the regular military and naval service of the United States. Hence, it requires none of the refinements of the tailor's art to build *out*, by ingenious artifices, striking and majestic shapes. The decadence, therefore, of the American officer as a social potentate, and his decline as a fascinating being in the eyes of womankind, is partially his own fault. Leaving home we find pride of the military person a matter of supreme interest abroad. Let the traveler recall the splendid *élan*, the active and finely drawn physique which marks the Imperial Guard of the Prussian army, where nearly every officer is a prince, and our own poverty of costume will become apparent. Is it to be marveled at that foreign critics of our habits, who for the first time behold an American military spectacle, make all manner of fun of the military tailoring displayed? Hence, furthermore, it is that we cut such a ridiculous figure in the painting, statuary, and great memorials, executed to commemorate the deeds of our great soldiers and sailors. It took Launt Thompson, one of the foremost artists of the world, over a year to pose and properly dress the figure of Admiral Dupont, which now stands in Washington as a bronze monument. No naval uniform of this day could be adapted to this quite recently deceased admiral, and great pains were necessary to prevent the bronze monument from becoming an unsightly heap of metal.

Nearly all of the battle pictures of the war as now painted offend the artistic eye, however they may be true to nature. Contrast the spirited and splendid color delineations of De Neuville and Détaille—in their canvasses exhibiting the carnage about Paris; or, in other works, the legions of Napoleon I returning from Moscow, or the triumphant entry of the French Imperial staff into Milan after the battle of Magenta—with those pictures of our own civil struggle—Fredericksburg, Manassas, and Vicksburg—and one can perceive how far behind we are in what every army should have—dramatic military effect. Therefore, whatever can be said of the fighting qualities of some of the noted militia regiments of New York and other cities of the Union, *pro* or *con*, they, at least, deserve—those we have in mind—high praise for their efforts to reform the uniforms of our soldiery. As to the regular service, a speedy and complete change could be made by the single signature of the Cabinet officer at the head of the service, and it is to be hoped he will not long delay. Nor would an autocratic mandate like this have other than a happy influence on civilian wear. Those who do not look beyond their noses cannot trace the influence of miltary wear on civil clothes; yet it exists, and always has been felt, and will continue to have a legitimate effect. The costume, however, and for whatever worn, has an undoubted dominion, extending beyond its immediate use, and from this fact and cognate causes we may look for the ultimate daily suit of clothes that will govern the new period in dress of the age to be.

CHAPTER XVIII.

THE MAN-MAKER.

BULWER, who, in describing Pelham, was drawing his own portrait, has left some inimitable reflections, showing what a poetical and ambitious temperament will do for a natural-born coxcomb as this strange litterateur was. But, as he said of himself, " Under the affectations of foppery, and the levity of a manner almost unique for the effeminacy of its tone, I veiled an ambition the most extensive in its object, and a resolution the most daring in the accomplishment of its means." Yet vanity of dress was never absent from his mental make-up; and, with pen or voice, he was always fluent when descanting on the garb of a gentleman. He thought that the supreme excellence of coats was not to be *too* well made; that they should have nothing of the triangle about them ; that wrinkles behind should be carefully avoided; that the coat should fit exactly, but without effort. This, he held, could never be

the case where any padding, beyond a thick
sheet of buckram placed under the shoulder,
and sloping gradually away toward the
chest, could be admitted. The collar, too,
was an important point worthy of the closest
attention. He thought it should be low
behind, broad, short, and slightly rolled.
About the tail of the coat, it was not to be
broad or square on any account, save when
the figure was much too thin. "And," said
he, "no license of fashion can allow a man
of delicate taste to imitate the posterior luxu-
riance of a Hottentot; on the contrary, I
would lean to the other extreme, and think
myself safe in a swallow-tail." As to the
sleeve, it was Bulwer's axiom that anything
too tight about the wrist should be avoided in
men's wear, as this tendency would give a large
and clumsy appearance to the hand. As the
waistcoat is apparently the least observed
article in dress, the fact is lost sight of that
it influences the whole appearance more than
any one not profoundly versed in the habil-
imentary art would suppose. Besides, it is
the only main portion of the attire in which
we, as men, have a fine opportunity for a re-

fined and highly cultivated taste ; for, whatever the fashions as to trousers and coats,
the wearer has a wide range in waistcoats
from which to choose and balance any peculiarities of figure or local coloring. In this
respect he has almost a woman's license.
Take the richly colored and dotted cashmeres
of to-day, and they present quite as exquisite
and rich effects on the chest of man as can
be found on the bust of fashionable women.
Let the artistic fact, therefore, enter into the
mind of every gentleman and every tailor,
that it is by variations (often radical) in cut,
color, and fabric of the waistcoat, that the
human figure can be made to have many
attractive aspects. Some men must have ex-
panse of shirt-front, some must be clad in cloth
up to the collar-button, while just media
are suitable for others. The dressier among
the famous men of these later days have
generally selected a rich and ornate species
of vest ; but extreme caution has always
been observed that nothing tawdry and common should be permitted. Herein a gentleman, without being vulgar or ostentatious,
may follow his own taste, and make it as ex-

clusive as possible, while in all other garments he must advise with and follow the reigning styles. Trousers and braces, or suspenders, if the name be better liked, could in themselves make a chapter. While the use of suspenders is a sanitary problem, to a certain extent, no immutable law can be promulgated thereon. For mere outward effect they are, no doubt, a very admirable expedient; otherwise, there can be no question that they do, to some degree, check the free movement of the body, and at times impose a disagreeable burden on the shoulders. On some figures they are indispensable, particularly when the physique tapers almost in a straight line from the shoulders to the feet; but when a gentleman is built with hips that belong to the ideal man, then he can dispense with these accessories without impairing the general effect of his well-made trousers. In this matter of trousers, too, there are individual conceits which often must be respected. The thin man, the *genus* stalk, is particularly sensitive, lest his tubular clothes should be too slender; and, oh! how does the jelly-legged biped implore you to make graceful outlines! And then there is the possessor of a delicately shapen and aristo-cratic foot, even too small for a man already; what will he not suggest to further enhance its effeminacy? Sometimes he would have his trousers short, so as to develop the fine-ness of his *bas de soie*, or give them a spring at the bottom to show only the tips of his shoes.

In selecting his man-maker, the true gentle-man of fashion, and even he who does not concentrate any particular thinking on dress, should be careful to inquire as to the quality of his clothes. Novices can rarely tell at a first glance goods of fine and superior manu-facture from those of inferior and fraudulent grades. This is chiefly true in the misrepre-sentations that are made in passing off native for English fabrics! And here comes in the patriotic American, and says, " Why should we not make as good cloth as the British?" The answer is simply we do not, and the reason is obvious. England has for her market the entire world—all of the European continent and South America, and the West and East Indies, not to speak of the Canadas, while the United States are obliged to manufacture against this great competition, fortified by cheap labor, for the home consumption alone. This is no place to preach tariff, or anti-tariff, sermons; but America has ample protection, and is still unable to make satisfactory woolens to suit the highest classes of merchant tailoring. Notwithstanding the high tariff, however, both importers, like the author, and our manufacturers, are grievously swindled annually by that abundant class who have clothes made in England, and actually smuggled into the country by a variety of familiar devices. There are even broken-down gentlemen who have credit left in England with their tailors for hundreds of suits of clothes, and who receive them in a clandestine way at this and other ports, only to dispose of them at one-third their value, or place them in a pawn-shop as almost daily customers. This is a curious method of keeping the wolf from the door, yet there are several well-known illustrations of it in New York. It is entirely possible to follow such a bent for years; and easily, where tailors have been under contract for so much a year.   But this system does not prevail in America, and much less now in England than is generally supposed.   It is worthy of note, too, that Englishmen are beginning to send to New York for their clothes, which cost them three English prices,—only that they may take advantage of our superb cutters and fitters.

CHAPTER XIX.

AXIOMATIC TRUTHS FOR THE GENTLEMAN AND THE TAILOR.

WHILE the author has sought to avoid anything like shoppiness in the preparation of this treatise, and has sought to avoid any cheap and redundant display of technical knowledge, he feels, in carrying out the intent of this work, as announced in the introduction, that he should lay down some general rules for gentleman and tailor which, if followed, will result in very materially advancing the aim he has in view—artistic wear, and the prosperity of the craft.

FOR THE GENTLEMAN.

I. Never select a tailor because his prices are low. This is a commandment quite as important as that laid down by Thomas Jefferson, in his *Ten Rules of Life:* "Never buy a thing because it is cheap." You may rely upon it, that the more

you pay for an article of clothing, at a
tailor's whose reputation is number one,
the better will be the garment in all
particulars—in closeness of fitting, excellence of workmanship, and superior
cloth and trimmings. It is obvious that
the merchant who is allowed a liberal
margin of profit, and who has keen
competition in his own field, will look
after that which he produces under such
circumstances, with a greater pride and a
keener scrutiny, than he would if doing
a hap-hazard business.

II. Having selected your tailor, go to him for
advice, and carefully weigh it in the
choosing of goods and styles; but you
are not required to surrender any peculiar ideas of your own, without their
fallacy and impracticability are thoroughly demonstrated. By all means, be
not in too much haste to have your
clothes hurried through without the
necessary fitting. This is one of the be-
setting sins of the American. And remember, likewise, that whatever your de-

fective physique—do you fancy yourself
too short or too tall, too thin or too ro-
tund—with a suitable measure, once
obtained, you can always present a
favorable exterior.

III. You should have a complete wardrobe
at all times. If this be prepared with
care, and covering every occasion where
you are liable to be present, and adapted
to special lines of life, embracing games,
hunting, riding, driving, and yachting,
the cost will be very moderate to re-
plenish it from time to time, as circumstances may require; and often, with
ample precautions, it will last for years.
It is an illustration of this principle to
note that the Prince of Wales is entitled
to wear seventy different uniforms. The
estimate is rather under than overstated,
for he has a right to don seventeen military and volunteer uniforms alone, to
say nothing of the special costumes as-
sociated with his position as Great Stew-
ard of Scotland, Governor of the Charter
House, Lord of the Isles, President of

the Society of Arts, knight of some score
of orders, etc.

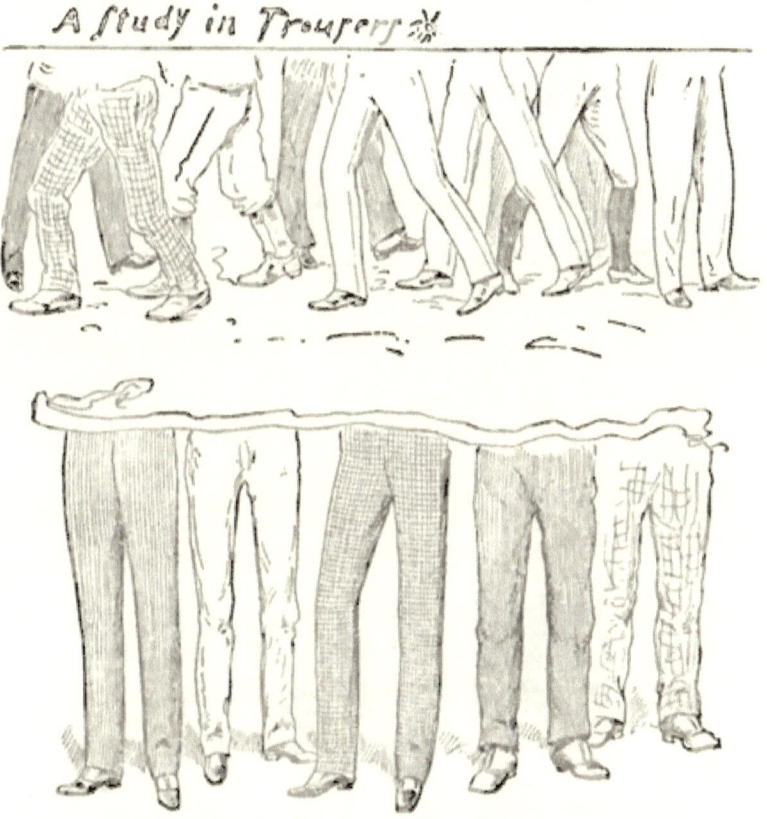

A Study in Trousers.

IV. Some flash and bizarre fashions should
be scrupulously avoided. There is
nothing so gratifying to the true gentleman as to be told that he is always well
dressed, without the observer's ability to

determine why. This result can easily be achieved by varying the garments, both as to pattern, figure, and colors, according to morning, evening, or dress occasions; and a not very extensive assortment is necessary for this purpose.

V. If you are a salaried man, and therefore one of method in your expenditures, set a fixed sum apart for dress, and even if this be seemingly large, you will find that a neat and otherwise attractive appearance will not militate against your advancement.

VI. Be scrupulous in observing the fixed laws of society, on public and dress occasions, in reference to your attire. Should you always be *en règle*, you will find yourself a welcome guest in many households and circles otherwise unattainable, and often in demand, from the sole fact, that you respect conventional forms and will never appear in an *outré* or ill-timed costume.

FOR TAILORS.

Tailors are often culpable sinners against their customers, and quite as often innocently so. But if, as a rule, they will follow these inflexible axioms, they will find themselves very soon on the high road to fortune, if the author can take his own modest successes as a criterion.

I. Promptitude should be the unfailing motto of every tailor, hoisted high above all others, to guide him in his journey through life. The author does not recall that he has ever, in a single instance, disappointed a customer, unless some unforeseen accident has occurred, and then the patron has been notified before the appointed time. More substantial business is gained by the strict observance of this duty, than by any intrinsic quality in the workmanship itself. That tailors have become a popular jibe for tardiness, unnecessary procrastination, and often downright lying, is due to carelessness in this particular. It may be set down as a just observation, that no proprietor

has a right to undertake to fill a definite
order for a fixed date, if he has any inward suspicion that he cannot execute it
on time.

II. At whatever pecuniary loss, no tailor
should permit a suit of clothes to issue
from his house if he has any doubts as
to its fitting or other qualities. To flat-
ter a patron into believing that he has
a splendid garment, by drowning his ex-
postulations with specious and technical
phraseology, or assuring him that it will
wear into the desired shape and ease, is
a kind of swindle which will travel fast,
to the tailor's injury. If an irremediable
misfit be made, better pocket the loss in
a good spirit, and with a lofty contempt
for a few paltry dollars, than send a man
out of your shop to be told by his
friends and rival cutters that you are a
slop-tailor.

III. Tailors should seek, by cultivating a
friendly rivalry among each other, to as-
sist, as a body, in praising good work

when it is seen, and avoiding unnecessary asperity in criticising those of high
standing in the guild. A really superior-
minded tailor is above any such prac-
tices as this, feeling that his work, like
that of the successful painter, speaks for
itself, where animadversions on the styles
or goods of others only have the effect to
confuse and bewilder the dressers, without any tangible advantage to any one.

IV. Above all, the present race of merchant
tailors should seek to throw around
dressing every artistic adjunct it is possible to secure. The servile copying of
the fashion plates and reproduction of
a suit of clothes worn by some European
notable are not the beginning and the
end of his science by any means. Rather
should he have an original turn to his
lines, if they do not offend the eye or the
rules of art, and place individual excellence in his designing as his ultimatum.

V. The customer should be constantly im-
pressed with this one truth — the better

his dress, the greater his popularity, the sounder his health, the more certain his prosperity and his daily reward of a life of content and happiness.

CHAPTER XX.

Count d'Orsay, undeniably the best dressed man of his time, held it for a maxim that in dress there was nothing insignificant. Nothing could be more true than this, and d'Orsay was himself a striking illustration of his saying. Those who saw him in the street or in the ball-room, at a reception or a review, carried away with them the impression of a radiant vision, a harmonious and admirable face and form, the detailed features of which they were wholly unable to describe, conscious only that everything was in its place and in keeping. This harmony was the result of a perfect art applied to a singularly fortunate nature; an art, that is, which neglected nothing in the details of the costume. If it had been otherwise, if d'Orsay could have worn an ill-fitting boot, or a hat that did not suit his dress, what a shock would have been given to the sensibilities of every observer! It is easy to apply the lesson taught by the example of this great leader of fashion.

Every man who can dress, owes it to society, to himself, to his tailor, to dress with care and attention to the smallest matters. There can be no greater or more fatal error than to imagine one's self fairly arrayed when coat, waistcoat, and trousers have been provided. As well imagine that a tree is perfect when it has trunk and branches and twigs, without either leaf or blossom or fruit. The neck-wear must be appropriate and refined, or the coat, though it be a masterpiece, will seem to have been unlawfully come by; the shirt-front must appear, not like a white sea, but so as to relieve the general effect of the upper costume; the cuffs must be of the right length, neither too long nor too short, either excess being destructive of the true function of the cuff, which is, to add a finish to the arm and tone down the abruptness of the transition from the sleeve of the coat to the hand, whether gloved or ungloved; and the boots must be without fault, easy, elegant in shape, and, as it were, the unavoidable and necessary outcome of the trousers.

There can be nothing accidental in a rightly dressed man. Each portion, each article of his outline, must be the continued expression of his individuality. This is no secret to the true tailor, but not every one has had the good fortune to put himself in the hands of an artist. So essential is attention to the smaller minutiæ of dress, that every intending patron of the art of costume should lay it down as a rule, for himself, never to think that he is dressed until his tailor has inspected and approved what has been done. There is even more in true attire than is yet suspected. All really permanent creations repose upon a solid basis of performance; a house must be founded upon the rock, and not upon the sand; a great painting, or a noble statue, implies long and patient study of principles and infinite labor in drawing, and so we hold it to be beyond the wit of man to dress well without a patient study and thoughtful arrangement of the underwear. The external fitness and elegance suppose an internal arrangement of corresponding qualities, and not to meet the expectation of this sincerity in apparel is to be guilty of a deep hypoc-

risy. Every reader of Ruskin remembers
with what burning eloquence this great genius
has denounced the shams of architecture, the
painted wood and iron in place of stone, the
molded stucco work where should have been
carved marble. If imitations like these are
detestable and immoral, what is to be said of
the fraudulent semblances made to do duty
in dress, which should be absolutely beyond
suspicion, seeing that it is the outward and
familiar shape by which a man is known alike
to friends and enemies? Who could endure
the thought of descending to put on what
the dictionaries call a *dickey?* The mind
shrinks back at the image brought before it,
and we hear with incredulity that good men
and true have masqueraded under this imperfect disguise. Good men they may have
been, in the sense of innocent, because ignorant and unthinking, men; but true men
they were not, for they went about among
their fellows with imposture in their thought,
and a shabby make-believe covering their
breasts. It is not thus that a really artistic
dress is to be made up or worn. In this,
sincerity and reality are the first requisites.

Beauty, in Plato's definition, is the fitness of things to their purpose; and he who would be well dressed must never forget this definition. The underwear must be of the best, and carefully fitted to the person; and, with this foundation well laid, the outer costume, designed by a true artist in his line, must give to every beholder the satisfaction of a perfect and rhythmical grace, and to the wearer the serenity of a mind and a conscience in harmony with the great law of right.* This may seem to be the language of exaggeration; but it is far from that. No man at ease with himself can be at war with the universe. Conduct, it has been said by a thoughtful writer, is three-fourths of human life; and right conduct in every human relation is at least three times as easy to the truly dressed man as it is to the unworthily attired. These things prove themselves.

---

* A long-continued personal experience enables the author to say, that Messrs. Webster Brothers, of 26 Lombard Street, London, have recognized this principle for years in cutting the drawers and shirts supplied by their house; and their attention to this point, so generally neglected, has recommended their products not less than the special quality of the gray wool employed.

It cannot be too carefully borne in mind
that the style of miscellaneous wear is a matter for serious study, with the counsel and
critical aid of the tailor. How far the personal peculiarities of the wearer ought to
modify his acceptance of the prevailing fashions is a question to which he himself can
hardly give a final answer; at least not until
that far-off day arrives for which Burns ut-
tered his still ungranted petition, that we
might

See oursels as ithers see us.

The tailor sees as the world sees, with an
added special intelligence entirely his own,
and his judgment should be the decisive one,
his approval the mint stamp on the coin.

Exaggerated style is the thing to be
avoided. It is right to be simple in taste,
but simplicity must not be carried too far,
lest it become conspicuous boldness; neither
should a prevailing fashion draw the eyes of
the passers-by to the fashion of the dress
rather than to the wearer of it. The extreme in either direction is an error, though
great examples may be brought forward to
justify each of these. How, for instance,

does the action of Brummel, when he made the crowd stare at his wonderful starched cravat, commend itself to the sound critic of costume? Only one answer is possible: it was a grave offense against the laws of good taste. This was one extreme. For an example of the other, take this passage, from a somewhat famous description of a distinguished Southern general, when about to address a great political meeting a few years ago: "His costume was characteristically simple; plain black, from head to foot, his waistcoat low cut, revealing the broad shirtbosom. *He was retiring in his neck-tie.*" The language is peculiar, but plain enough to show that the great soldier overstepped the modesty of true art in the studied simplicity, or, shall we say, the obtrusive withdrawal of his neck wear from public view? It had been less offensive to good dressing to appear without a neck-tie than with one which painfully attracted the eyes of all to its affectation. In all these matters the perfect model is Count d'Orsay, and every one who is happily endowed by nature may, with pains and study, approach to his excellence.

The constant study and effort to improve
are indispensable. One can never know too
much of the science and art of form, and also
of color. The real artist-tailor must have
a knowledge of the laws of color, to direct
and chasten his practical acquaintance with
the effects produced by juxtaposition and by
contrast. He can guide in the right way
those who would otherwise wander in con-
fusion of mind, but his task is lightened
when his customer has also paid attention to
this subject.

Chevreul on Color should be the hand-book
of every man of fashion. It is not, perhaps,
out of place, to suggest, while on the subject
of color, that the greater clearness and bright-
ness of the American sky must be allowed
for in studying contrasts and harmonies of
shade and tones originated under the duller
heaven of England.

If it is necessary to pay great attention to
the finish and proportion of the collars, and
other visible portions of the underwear, it is
quite as imperative to give long and anxious
thought to the gloves, the shoes, and the jewelry, which cannot be an after-thought. The

simple rule for the gloves and the shoes is the French one, to be *bien chaussé et bien ganté*. Nothing can be added to this, for it covers the whole field. One needs only to remember that the hands are made to lay hold of and to relinquish objects, and the feet to walk with and to support worthily the state-ly form of manhood. The gloves, therefore, should cover, not cramp the fingers. If prop-erly fitted, they give an air of their own to the hands, and leave them, at the same time, free for all the courtesies of life.

It is the same with the boots or the shoes. The shoes that pinch belittle and degrade the wearer more than any other solecism in dress. It is in vain that a man with shoes too small for him endeavors to appear well dressed. His clothes may be masterpieces, but the attention will be perversely drawn to his hobbling gait and the attempted disguise that disguises nothing. The shoe must fit the well-dressed man, and it is the perfection of its fit that will make it seem to be even smaller than its actual measure. Every at-tempt at deceiving the eyes of others in this part of the dress is hopeless, and the unlucky wearer of too small shoes has not even the satisfaction of a self-delusion like that of the ostrich with his head in a bush; for he sees that every one sees his flimsy imposture.

Should a well-dressed man wear jewelry? This question suggests, like many other questions, the need of a new word to meet the necessities of a new development in social customs. For want of a better, we are obliged to call by the vague and inappropriate name of jewelry the watch-chain, the ring, and one or two minor articles of gold and precious stones which a gentleman now permits himself to wear. As a received part of the costume, what is properly known as jewelry is unheard of. The days are gone when a great noble could present himself in society in a coat blazing with diamonds, so loosely sewn on that every now and then some of them fell to the floor, to be the prize of the first comer. Gone, too, not to return in our day, the time when Disraeli, in the beginning of his career as novelist and man of fashion and politician, dazzled the eyes of London with his semi-barbaric richness of ornament. In that time even the sober citizen of London, and the American, with his confessedly limited and provincial ambitions, held it to be beneath the dignity of a respectable man to appear in public without the bunch of seals attached to his massive watch-guard. Where are now those solid cubes of gold, set with red and white carnelians and dark cairngorms, dangling to and fro, or reposing trustfully against the person, according to the wearer's greater or lesser breadth of beam? Who can find them? Who can gather up the snows of the past winter?

To-day there is a changed spirit abroad. A chain, the less noticeable the better, a ring, and by preference a seal-ring, wrist-buttons, and a scarf-pin, make up the jewelry in the attire of a well-dressed man. Of all these the seal-ring is undeniably the one with the noblest pedigree and the least questionable title. The watch is of comparatively recent origin, and, even if we regard it as indispensable to the personal outfit, may well be worn without the golden chain, while it is quite conceivable that a severer taste may repudiate the scarf-pin as unnecessary, or even as the sign of a harking-back toward barbarism;

but the seal-ring is identified with the very principle of civilization. It is the symbol of law, of the respect for constituted authority, of the sacredness of contracts, of the responsibilities, in one word, which hold society together. In no one article that is worn is there concentrated so much of personal character and dignity as in the seal-ring, consecrated, as it has been from the earliest ages, to the most serious and solemn purposes and to the gravest occasions in the life of its owner. How much of the unwritten history of the race partly reveals itself in the collections of seals in our museums! A well-cut seal is in itself an evidence of its wearer's identity and an expression of the refinement and solidity of his culture.

CHAPTER XXI.

THE PROPOSED REVOLUTION IN DRESS.

WHEN Louis the Sixteenth was talking with the Duke de la Rochefoucauld-Liancourt on the night after the taking of the Bastille, he wound up his remarks with the words: "It is an insurrection." "No, sire," replied the duke, "It is a revolution." The leaders of fashion, like the rulers of kingdoms, often mistake the signs of the times, and fail to appreciate the gravity of a situation which is the result of causes not actually within the range of sight. To pronounce the word *revolution* is to alarm and disconcert the vast multitude whose belief in the permanence of existing conditions is absolute. It may be a consolation to some to remind them that the revolution is always with us, like the poor, like the succession of day and night. In the cycles of style and of fashion, as in those of the natural world, movement is the supreme law, and movement around a central point. As in language, so in dress. Many forms that have gone down will rise again, and others, now held in honor, will pass away.

Is there to be a revolution in styles of dress? No one can say when such an event is near at hand, still less can any one hope to bring it about by preaching or even by example, except in the modification of existing forms, and this is not revolution, but change. Too ambitious an aim in such matters surely defeats itself, even when led by an acknowledged authority and power, like that of the Prince of Wales. When undertaken by a lesser man, ridicule gathers about the movement and overwhelms the leader and his followers. This is seen in the history of Oscar Wilde's proposed reform, a scheme not intrinsically absurd, and not without good features of its own, but mismanaged from the beginning, because its apostle was deficient in a sense of humor, and, one cannot help thinking, more or less insincere. There must be singleness of purpose in the advocate of reform, and the purpose must be a worthy one. Self-seeking must be far from his thought, and even the suspicion of it must be avoided.

So far as an outlook over the broad field

can reassure us, we may feel that no very great change in costume is to be expected in the near future. The democratic spirit of the age, and the constantly widening commercial activities of every people, are mighty influences at work to limit and define the general style of dress in the world. It is becoming more and more difficult to assign a man to his place in society on the evidence of his costume, and this state of things will last for a long time to come. There will always be the distinction between the well-dressed man and the man who is careless of his attire; but the number of the well-dressed will go on increasing with the spread of sound information and the growth of right ideas, and, with added numbers, the better dressed portion of the people will constantly attract to themselves more recruits from the less advanced multitude. It will only be when something like an equilibrium is reached, when the world is about fairly divided between the two, that a revolution will have everything in its favor.

The growth of taste in art, and especially in painting and sculpture, is working silently

and surely to modify the views of men with regard to costume. So long as the business world
is the all-important world, the conceptions of
the end and aim of dress must be shaped, in
part, at least, by the needs of business. The
principle of Herbert Spencer, that man is the
result of his conditions and his environment, is
decisive in this matter. Even if we would, we
cannot escape from the controlling powers and
forces of the time. The day will come, however, when a knowledge of art, and the famil-
iarity with the great artistic periods of history, will have made men impatient of the poverty of modern attire in the picturesque and
æsthetic elements, neglect of which for too long
a time is sure to revenge itself upon the intellectual nature and diminish the creative
forces of a people.* Illustrations of this truth
are to be found nearer home than China, but
there is no one country that supplies the illustration on a scale so vast. Thorough and
perfect in detail as is the art of China, it is a

---

* The revolt has begun in Germany, where the artists of
Düsseldorf and of Dresden have discarded the costume of
the present age and have returned to the picturesque style of
the days of Rubens, the black velvet breeches with blue
stockings, the velvet vest, trimmed with red silk, and the
large felt hat with or without plumes.

stereotyped and immobile art, the continued reproduction of the same models and the same forms. Stricken with sterility at an early day, from whatever cause, the Chinese might be said to have no apprehension of the picturesque, were it not for their landscape-gardening. In every other direction their intellectual nature, keenly alive to material and practical aims, bears the unmistakable impress of the prosaic, and this is not only a great defect, it is also the source of incalculable positive loss to the productive power of the nation. Natural genius has, of course, something to do with this effect; but the imaginative gift has been bestowed upon all races, and the ancient inventions of the Chinese show that they at one time possessed it in no small measure. What they are to-day other peoples may well shrink from becoming; nor has any one of them reason to fear such a future, so long as it keeps alive the divine fire on the altars of art. This will purify the atmosphere of our modern world, and no other single agency can do so much for us. Every form of art, architecture, painting, sculpture, music, engraving, carving,

cameo and gem-cutting, must be made familiar to us, not only in the products in our
shops and stores and homes, but in the importance given to them in our educational
systems and our libraries. The spirit that
craves this intellectual gratification is the
spirit that creates salutary, because æsthetic,
revolutions in costume, but it must be a spirit
animating a whole people. When the change
is at hand it will announce itself surely
enough, so that men will not be left unguided
to wander after false teachers; but we may
well speculate to some profitable purpose on
the direction a revolution of the kind will
take.

Is it likely that the movement will be slow
and tentative, or rapid and decided? Established usage, and the enormous inter-
ests involved, lead us to accept more readily
the idea of a gradual retrogression toward a
period not too far remote, beginning with the
single step of a change of form in some one
article, such as the coat, or the waistcoat, and
passing on from that to another, until the
whole scheme of dress is transformed. This
is what seems at first sight the orderly devel-

WILL IT EVER COME TO THIS?

opment of the idea of reform in a matter so
settled as to its main characteristics; but is
it quite certain that reforms, beginning as

this one would, from the people, would follow this orderly progression?

There are historical examples of reform in
dress imposed upon the nation by the will of
the ruler, and against great opposition; but
these are hardly of a nature to help us to a
conclusion. The severe garb prescribed by
Calvin, for the people of Geneva, was accepted
in a religious temper of mind not less austere
than his own, while it needed all the despotism
of Peter, and all the sacred character of his
authority in the eyes of his subjects, to carry
out his decrees against the national costume,
and the no less national beard; nor could any
will less stubborn than that of Mahmoud II
have forced upon his fanatical people and
army the detested uniform of the Franks.
On the other hand, we find the Japanese
ready to adopt, with the sciences and the arts
of the West, the costume that seems at first
to make a sharp division between the European and the Oriental. In a movement for
reform in dress in America, are we likely to
show ourselves more or less conservative than
the Japanese? Our errors are more likely to
be on the side of conservatism. It was

rather the sense of a national inferiority, in obvious respects, that made the Japanese hasten to abandon the civilization of their fathers to take up that of the West. Nothing like this can influence the American, for, in all that pertains to the material advantages of the highest civilization, he is in line with the foremost, and the leaven of culture in all that makes the older countries of the Christian world attractive is working more actively with every year on a larger number of people in the United States. Substantially the same with the people of the Old World, the Americans have the advantage over them that all the inspiring associations, all the witchery and charms of travel in the storied lands of Europe, are new and fresh to the visitor from the New World, and impress him with an abiding sense of their infinite value. Great historic scenes, castles and palaces, and august ruins, he cannot transplant to his Western home; but the faces and figures of the men who gave immortal renown to these famous places haunt his recollection and mingle with his dreams of the future, that his children are to see.

What more natural than that this noiseless and pervading influence of culture, which already declares itself in the architecture of the land, should one day bring about a general and spontaneous movement for a revival in America of the picturesque and stately costume of the heroic Elizabethan age? There is needed for such a revival a public, weary of the tame monotony that fills our streets; and this public is gathering power and volume with every year that passes over us. Who, that has looked upon a procession in one of our great cities, has not felt that dullness and common-place are more formidable in the out-door life of America than elsewhere in the world? The military music stirs the blood as it does in Europe; but while in Europe the feeling for beauty is gratified by the varied and splendid costumes, no less than by the brilliant uniforms of the soldiers marching past, our processions are made up in far too large a proportion of citizens in the every-day dress that permits no illusion in the mind of the spectator. While the Marseillaise, or Beethoven's Turkish March, is thrilling through the veins, the eyes rest on a line of six or seven hundred John Smiths, in black coats, walking in the middle of the street, for their own satisfaction, possibly, but not for the entertainment of others.

There must be an end to this kind of thing, as the perception of the significance of art becomes clearer. The colorless aspect of American life is not the natural outcome of the conditions made for us in a land so full of light and beauty, and we may well rest content with the belief in the power of the imagination to bring out the latent love of form in a people that inherits so fully the tendencies and the traditional impulses of the great races of the world.

For the American takes kindly to culture. Active and energetic as he is in the pursuit of business, he is rarely unobservant of the finer possibilities that lie beyond success. The minor courtesies of life come to him as if by instinct, and one is surprised to see with how little friction the business of the day proceeds among men so eager and so intent upon their own objects. With natures so receptive of the finer influences from without, the Americans are singularly fitted to begin the reaction against the prosaic in dress; a reaction that must come with the increase of wealth and noble leisure, and the love of those liberal arts which soften and dignify the manners and adorn the life of man.

It is enough to believe that the future will be at least equal to the past ages in the creation of variety and picturesqueness in costume. There will be new conditions made, and new adaptations and combinations of older forms to meet the requirements of the coming time; and, firm in this faith, the author closes this survey of the field, that has so much engaged his attention and his serious thought, like one who feels that

> 'tis a joy to straighten out
> One's limbs, and leap elastic from the counter,
> Leaving the petty grievances of earth,
> The breaking thread, the din of clashing shears,
> And all the needles that do wound the spirit.

www.ingramcontent.com/pod-product-compliance
Lightning Source LLC
Chambersburg PA
CBHW020614030726
47497CB00007B/2236